C.P. SURENDRAN is a poet and novelist. He was former editor-in-chief of DNA. He is also a columnist for Indian and international journals. He lives in Delhi.

Also by C.P. Surendran

POETRY

Gemini II (1994)
Posthumous Poems (1999)
Canaries on the Moon (2002)
Portraits of the Space We Occupy (2007)

FICTION

An Iron Harvest (2006)
Lost and Found (2010)
Hadal (2015)

SCREENPLAY

Gour Hari Dastaan: The Freedom File (2015)

Available Light

New and Collected **POEMS**

C.P. Surendran

SPEAKING
TIGER

SPEAKING TIGER PUBLISHING PVT. LTD
4381/4, Ansari Road, Daryaganj
New Delhi 110002

Published in India by Speaking Tiger in paperback 2017

Copyright © C.P. Surendran 2017

ISBN: 978-93-86702-83-8
eISBN: 978-93-86702-81-4

10 9 8 7 6 5 4 3 2 1

Typeset in Goudy Old Style by SÜRYA, New Delhi
Printed at Sanat Printers, Kundli

All rights reserved.
No part of this publication may be reproduced,
transmitted, or stored in a retrieval system,
in any form or by any means, electronic,
mechanical, photocopying, recording
or otherwise, without the prior
permission of the publisher.

This book is sold subject to the condition that it shall not,
by way of trade or otherwise, be lent, resold,
hired out, or otherwise circulated, without the
publisher's prior consent, in any form of
binding or cover other than that in
which it is published.

*To those whom I served grief
In killer cups; raged naked and free
As the first man to their disbelief
Consider these words olive; fig leaf to me.*

CONTENTS

Foreword: A Suture for a Sacred Wound	xix
Riding the Horse of Life to Death: A Tribute	1

From *Available Light*

A Note to the Self from Tranquebar	11
Dolomedes Tenebrosus: Spontaneous Male Death	13
Headcount	14
House Hunting	15
Hadal	16
Mirtaz, Daxid, Zapiz	17
Journey	
Wipes	18
Damage	18
Mask	19
Omen	19
Couple	20
Signature	21
Shakti Mills	22
Wordless	23
Two	24
Dhobi Ghat	25

Connected	26
Four Figures of Speech	
Serial Killer	27
Voyage	27
Steam	28
Unborn	28
Retro	29
The End of an Affair	30
Installation	31
Marxists	32
Engagement	33
What the Doctor Said	34
Cowboy	35
Mirrors	36
Justice	37
Defiance	38
Repeat Radio	39
Absolute	40
Prophecy	41
Hoopster	42
Graveyard Shift	
Self-recrimination	43
Lodi Garden, Winter	43
Monotony in NY	44
Conversation with a Nine-Year-Old on God, Devil, and Life after Death	45

Erasure
- Drain — 46
- Water Colour — 46
- Passage — 47
- Third Person Singular — 47
- Memorabilia — 48
- Incest — 48
- Disconnection — 49
- Solo — 49
- Mismatch — 50
- Last Supper — 50

Morning Glory — 52

A Promise in South Sudan — 53

S.O.S — 54

Phantoms
- Reflection — 55
- Bender — 56
- The Departed — 56
- Spooked — 57

Apocalypse — 58

Weather—and Other—Reports — 59

False — 60

Diadem — 61

Umbilical Cord — 62

Pawn — 63

Still Life	64
Umbrellas in Hong Kong	65
Sparrows	66
Day	67
Night	68
Double Decker	70
The Plain of Jars	71
There Was a Man in the Land of Uz	72
Grace: Woman Metalling Road	75
An Act in November	76
As Kill a King	77
David, Don't Be Sad, That Was a Dream	
Selection	78
Kristallnacht	80
Witness	82
Regiment	82
Once Upon a Time	83
Vein	83
Lingua Tertii Imperii	84
Boy Who Saw No Tree, Bird, Star	84
The Twilight of the Gods	85
Jukebox in Colaba	86
Washing	87
Ka-Be	87
Prayer	88

Harbinger	89
Gospel	90
Yana	91
Ledger	91
The Time of Our Lives	92
This Close	93
Clean Is Good	93
Heart	94
Bridge	95
Prize	95
Invitation	96
Tracers	97
Quiet	97
Last Season	98
Arrivals, Departures	99
Good Friday	99
Available Light	101
Price	102

From *Portraits of the Space We Occupy*

Primary Colour	105
Design	106
The Sowing Circle	107
Luminous	110
Catch	111

Line of Fire	112
Alchemy	113
Bombay	
Highway	114
Professional	114
Down at Heel	115
Conflagration	116
Out of Joint	116
Sidewalk Art Plaza	118
Prospect	119
Ruhnama	
Works	120
Praise	120
Benediction	121
Penance	122
Global Warning	123
Red Tape	123
Bollywood	124
External Affairs	125
Thrift: A Letter to the Mayor	125
Drop Out	126
Curriculum Vitae	126
A Shortage of Words	128
Catafalque	
Post Natal	130

Eclipse	131
Favour	131
Threshold	132
Rout	132
Permanent Revolution	133
Pogrom	134
Chutney and Gruel	135
I Spy	136
I	136
Oedipus Vexed	137
Post Crypt	138
Statue	138
Homage to a Hen	139
Dog	139
Face to Face	140
Full Circle	140
Portraits of the Space We Occupy	141
Boy	142
Sound Proof	142
Gastronomy	142
Vision	143
Who Shifts the Stars So June Is Here Again?	143
Guest	144
Translation	144

From *Canaries on the Moon*

Extraterrestrial	147
A Drop	148
A Necessary War	150
Season Flipping	152
Parli	
Exile and the Kingdom	153
Daze	153
Asthma	154
Replenishment	155
Blow by Blow Account of a Boy Missing	155
Soldier	156
A Quick Brown Fox	156
Bless and Curse	157
Coffee	158
Passover	159
Each King in His Place	160
Statistics	161
A Nightmare	163
Dire	
Bat	165
Parody	165
Futile	166
Pause	167
Cambridge, Autumn	167
Kalki Brimming	167

Stone	168
News in Brief	169
Reading Glasses	170
Aasa Khosa	170
Waiting	171
Rumour	172

From *Posthumous Poems*

Toast	177
Night Vision	178
The Family Court	179
Goal Keeper	180
Return	181
Anchored by a Hare's Breath	182
Thief	183
Dedication	184
War and Peace	185
In Good Company	186
Contentment	187
Tea	188
Cargo	189
Afterwards	190
Forgetting the Dark	191
Ghost	192
Question: Do You Have Nightmares?	193

The Colours of the Season's Best Dream	194
Beauty	196
What van Gogh Meant	197
Beauty Parlour	199
Happily Living Ever Laughter	200
Marine Drive	201
Mirror in Blizzard When Lights Went Out	202
Starters	203
A Cold Feeling	204

From *Gemini II*

Low Life	
Click	207
Curios	207
A Friend in Need	208
Shopping	208
Catch-22	209
Invisible Man	209
A Visit to the Countryside	210
Milk Still Boils	210
Morning Show	211
Demolition	212
Departure	213
Roadshow	214
Elusive	215

Renunciation	216
Movie	217
Sunrise in Bed	218
Retard	219
Malabari	
Out of My Window	220
Inspiration	220
Zamorin	221
Piscina	221
Legacy	222
Sunday Morning Jerk Off	224
Annunciation	225
Annunciation II	226
Witch	227
Loose Ends	228
First Signs, Last Rites	229
Requiem of the Rose	230
Lazarus	231
Back	232
Saturday Poems	
War	233
Travel	233
Harmony	234
Marked	235
Documentary	236

Dire	237
Stranded	238
Immortals	239
Acknowledgements	241

FOREWORD

A Suture for a Sacred Wound

C.P. Surendran does not entertain an unduly optimistic belief in the human animal's ability to redeem itself from its failings. The universe of his poems demonstrates a cyclic rhythm: it alternates between brief redemptive moments of insight and resistance on the one hand, and the gratuitous violence and melancholy self-flagellation that more typically define the human condition, on the other.

C.P.'s awareness of the suffering that falls to humankind's lot echoes the cadences of the Order for the Burial of the Dead from the Anglican *Book of Common Prayer*, 1662: 'Man that is born of a woman hath but a short time to live, and is full of misery. He cometh up, and is cut down, like a flower; he fleeth as it were a shadow, and never continueth in one stay.' Locating the individual on a scale of evolutionary possibilities that combines a pragmatic Darwinism with a residual theology, he recognizes our constant struggle to be 'something more than the apes', even as we manage to be 'something less than the angels'.[1]

This struggle is accentuated by the elusiveness of that traditional source of radiance and consolation: the Divine. In 'There Was a Man in the Land of Uz', a poem resonant with Biblical cadences, C.P. addresses his *Deus absconditus*:

> Invisibly inked, your writs are mysteries,
> Unravelled by the sun and, as often the moon, mostly sad
> As infants who never saw light; the cruelty of it all
> Pointless as a bomb dropped in an anatine pond,
> Numbing as the mother sundered from her child,
> No matter what Eliphaz, Bildad or Zophar try
> To say in your praise and win your case.

The prime mover of cosmic and individual destinies remains inscrutable, manifest only through unpredictable, inexplicable, catastrophic blows aimed at the innocent. C.P.'s recent poetry is informed by a shifting, Manichean interplay between light and darkness, belief and doubt, affirmation and lament: his key trope, enshrined in the title of this substantial collection of his new and previous poems, is that of 'Available Light'. I find myself asking what the sources of such illumination might be: natural, as in the sun and moon he invokes in the poem from which I have just quoted; or artificial, as in his late-night or early morning confrontations with fate, foible or circumstances; or, as we may divine from the poems in which he addresses such historical tragedies as the Holocaust, the interrogator's lamp? Or perhaps C.P.'s *Available Light* is some combination of all these, as experienced in a space of confinement or concealment.

The poet himself recalls the term from its use by Satyajit Ray in an interview with Shyam Benegal; the legendary filmmaker told his younger contemporary in the world of cinema that the factor of available light, modulated through a system of reflectors into bounce light, had opened up and marked out the 'possibilities of realism' for him. C.P. associates the term, also, with Henri Cartier-Bresson's idea of taking photographs in natural light, without recourse to artificial devices such as the flash, which he likened to using a pistol in church. 'And, of course,' says C.P. ruefully, 'the supply of light grows smaller as we grow older.'[2] For me, the phrase is forever associated with the influential cultural anthropologist Clifford Geertz's last book, *Available Light: Anthropological Reflections on Philosophical Topics* (2000), a collection of essays that testify to their author's practice of combining a salutary *skepsis* and an enduring empathy in his lifelong study of culture, those 'webs of significance' that human beings produce together. Ray, Cartier-Bresson, Geertz—all these emphases are relevant to our mapping of C.P.'s journey.

The Bombay of the late-1980s was hospitable to a number of young poets who were beginning to make their way in the world; we were working on what would become our first manuscripts while also finding a berth in the domains of cultural journalism, academia, or the visual arts. I first met C.P. at the offices of the afternoon newspaper, *Mid-day*, where I had gone to meet Jeet Thayil; we had read together at Meher Pestonjee's salon in Colaba the previous evening, and he had offered to publish my poems on the cultural page that he edited. C.P. was Thayil's colleague on the editorial staff. He seemed to have placed himself at a distinct angle to the world; although this, in itself, would have occasioned no surprise, since all of us were pursuing tangents of various kinds from the conventional stabilities of life. What distinguished C.P. was that he seemed to be robed in an impenetrable despondency. Later, I would learn that he was recovering from the collapse of his first marriage, which his wife had unilaterally ended after moving to USA. I would get to know C.P. well and our camaraderie and friendship continued across other contexts—newspaper offices, poetry readings, literary festivals—and eventually *The Times of India* group, where we both worked for a number of years.

I have attempted elsewhere—in the Introduction to Dom Moraes' *Selected Poems*—to convey something of the cartography of our lives in those years, the places we inhabited, the mentor figures who played a vital role in our formation:

> By the late 1980s, the orbit of Anglophone poetry in Bombay could be mapped around three major centres of gravity: Nissim Ezekiel's book- and paper-strewn office at the PEN All-India Centre, on New Marine Lines, near Churchgate Station; Adil Jussawalla's apartment at Cuffe Parade, or the offices of the various journals for which he acted, successively, as literary or features editor; and Dom Moraes' apartment at Sargent Road, Colaba, or the Sea Lounge at the Taj Mahal Hotel, Apollo Bunder, where he would arrange to meet people by appointment. Young poets hoping to be received into a larger tradition, or more mundanely to receive criticism or find avenues for publication, found their way to one or the other, and rarely all three, of the figures who comprised this impressive troika.[3]

Even at this time, it was clear that C.P.'s practice was strongly premised on the candour of a personal life that is exposed and examined, sometimes pitilessly. In his poetry, as in his novels, non-fiction, columns, essays and film work, the individual is pitted against a hostile world—he is not heroic in the grand manner so much as he is a self-doubter who must survive both the world and his own self-destructive impulses towards frenzy or despair. In such a predicament, poetry might serve as a lifeline, a possibility of understanding if not also healing. This is what I wrote about him in 2002, in the Introduction to a Viking anthology I edited, *Reasons for Belonging: Fourteen Contemporary Indian Poets*:

> For C.P. Surendran, whose insistent abruptness of rhythm barely contains a deep-welling, anguished rage, poetry is a security perimeter guarding the consciousness against the siege warfare of intimate relationships and social arrangements, the random strikes of destiny. Poetry is a promise of the recovery of wholeness after trauma for Surendran, a covenant of resurrection; in 'Starters', he achieves a rich fusion of the sacred and the profane in the briefest of strokes:
>
> > I reach for my first drink,
> > The fountain flowing out of my head,
> > Dark ink.[4]

The early C.P. adopted a bohemian self-image, a radically nihilist attitude towards the world. He was ready to embrace catastrophe. He was committed to colliding with the world. Thinking back to this period in an email conversation, he recalls, 'What troubled me about myself was my sense of doom. I am not quite sure where I got it from. There is a poem I've written about my asthma. They had given me up for dead when I was forty days old, because my face had gone completely blue. And then miraculously I was able to breathe again. I trace my sense of death and foreboding to that event; also the delusion that I am all alone. It's a little like Lazarus. How to tell what happened? My essential nature is adversarial. I don't find the world a hospitable place. After all it had given me up for dead!'[5]

In considering C.P.'s sources and inspirations, and contextualizing his work, I find myself revisiting his complex, ambivalent and conflicted relationship with his father, the celebrated rationalist and Left-wing Malayalam writer Pavanan (1925-2006). Over the years, C.P.'s attitude towards his father and his generation of writers, with their undimmed faith in Communism, has undergone a shift from adversarial critique to empathetic acceptance. 'Most of my young life was not well directed, and I had taken to alcohol at a rather young age. For a long time, and unreasonably, I held my father responsible for all of it. He was the president of the Kerala Rationalist Association for some twenty years, a very active Kerala Sahitya Akademi chief for a long time, a great chronicler of Kerala in the 1960s and '70s, a great critic, too,' says C.P. 'To be fair, I think I was an ingrate. My revolt with myself must have spilled over all around, and I must have hurt my father a great deal. I remember once his coming over to Bombay while I was doing a series of *Sunday Review* columns called "Low Life". He happened to read one of them—the *Times* was not easily available in Kerala then—and urged me not to continue with it, because he found it too painful to read. In retrospect, I still am not clear if my revolt was against him or what he represented: Malayalam and its strange and, with some exceptions, rather conformist literature; his terrifying optimism in the very human project of the enterprise of meaning, his circle of great writers and political leaders, who had all suffered political repression and come out of it smiling. The underground Communist movement in my father's young days had a terrible time.'[6]

The C.P. of the present is more measured in his approach to the world, less welcoming of apocalyptic destinies. Shock has had its day. It no longer forms a major part of his repertory; instead, his writing is marked by a recognition of the seesaw between atomization and solidarity, on which the individual must balance: 'I don't believe in constructed identities like the nation. I do believe that I am empathetic as well; why else do I find myself writing for the wretched underdog?'[7] In another exchange of communications that we had last year, C.P. reflected: 'It does seem to me that the first half of my poetry is a way to come to terms with the shock of one's birth. The second seems to be an attempt at fleeing death. In between somewhere there is the social world to deal with. And the *word* complicates that too.'[8]

Even as we acknowledge language as the carrier of an intensely private articulation, we also know it to be an abundantly, sometimes overwhelmingly and self-defeatingly social medium of communication; we know, too, that language can be brutalized, turned to an instrument of hate, viciousness, demagoguery, and annihilatory rhetoric. In the present collection, C.P. includes a long sequence of poems titled 'David, Don't Be Sad, That Was a Dream', bulletins of terror and nightmare charged with the memory of *Kristallnacht* and the Holocaust, electric with the fear of a world that might rapidly turn into a concentration camp or a death camp. C.P.'s long-term devotion to the work of Primo Levi and Paul Celan, both survivors of the Holocaust who were devastated by the experience and eventually took their own lives, is manifest here. One of the 'David' poems takes its title from the title of a great memoir of those dark times, written by the German Jewish philologist and professor of French literature Victor Klemperer and published in 1947 from notes he had preserved while under the threat of extinction: *Lingua Tertii Imperii: Notizbuch eines Philologen*, or *The Language of the Third Reich: A Philologist's Notebook*.

Nazism, Klemperer writes, 'permeated the flesh and blood of the people through single words, idioms and sentence structures which were imposed on them in a million repetitions and taken on board mechanically and unconsciously. ... Words can be like tiny doses of arsenic: they are swallowed unnoticed, appear to have no effect, and then after a little time the toxic reaction sets in after all.'[9] C.P.'s homage to the victims of the colossal evil of Nazism, 'Lingua Tertii Imperii', reads, in its entirety:

> The night at the edge of knife
> Extends remembrance endlessly.
> How they ran round and round

In enormous shoes
Of thorn, how they looked forever
For the ice of what's gone;
How the earth shook
Under thrones;
How a bullet emptied
Them of the earth.
How from helmets grass sprung
Again in innocence of pain.
How language,
Leashed to that place and time,
Barked and growled,
And Cerberus understood.

The invocation of the canine guardian of the Greek netherworld leads us to C.P.'s favourite adjective in recent years: 'Hadal', concerning Hades as well as the depths of the ocean, which was the title of C.P.'s third novel, cast in the armature of the classic spy thriller and published in 2015. In C.P.'s telling, the netherworld is here and now: it extends itself through fugitive experiences, the ambiguities of selfhood, the betrayal of others. The oceanic depths, too, are within us: implacable, atavistic energies burst up from unknown depths within us, driven by our fears, compelling us to serve a sovereign and ruthless will to compete, survive and flourish; compelling us to instrumentalize feelings and relationships as we permit conditions of extremity to distort and deform the self. 'Hadal' is also the title of one of his recent poems, which reads as follows:

> The waves white with what they witnessed
> Below return, bowing and scraping
> Along the shadows they throw
> On shore; back,
> Back to the silence thick as massed glass,
> To first fish, time cutting teeth in the dark;
> Ossified bones, hermaphrodite flesh, marine snow.

> The cold is without thought. Things alive
> Barely breathe. Your body sieves the sun
> To the last. Here you are: in your element,
> Feeding the sea out of your hand;
> The memory-pumping heart is salt.
>
> The sands rise from your pores,
>
> There the shadows start.

If the *Book of Common Prayer* suggests that we flee as shadows, C.P. sees us as revenant shadows, hurled back from the depths with sediments of knowledge and self-knowledge, animated by salt and water, drowned, broken, made whole again. One possible way of characterizing C.P.'s career is to view it as a harrowing pilgrimage through a world in which the poet is both participant and observer, sometimes a barely tolerated insider but most often an outsider deciphering and decoding the structures of relationship, identity, belonging, neighbourhood, and community. While it is customary to regard alienation as a negative and disabling condition, might we consider the possibility that it is, in fact, often a productive condition, offering us emancipation from the burden of representing or subscribing to a system, and disclosing insights that might otherwise have been concealed beneath the normalization of social and political processes? Indeed, as the anthropologist and anarchist thinker David Graeber argues, 'The idea that alienation is a bad thing is a modernist problem. Most philosophical movements—and, by extension, social movements—actually embrace alienation. You're trying to achieve a state of alienation. That's the ideal if you're a Buddhist or an early Christian, for example: Alienation is a sign that you understand something about the reality of the world.'[10]

In this spirit, C.P. bears witness to derelict polyphonies of affect, animates them into a condition of *sayability*, steering them towards what must be *written*: testimony, testament to what James Agee memorably described as 'the cruel radiance of what is'. Anyone who looks directly at that 'cruel radiance' is very likely to be wounded; for the poet is not only a pilgrim in a dangerous landscape but also a trespasser in secluded zones—psychic, cultural or political—that would prefer to guard their mysteries. As in Greek mythology, the guardian of such a sanctuary, usually a serpent or a dragon, inflicts a wound on the trespasser who has entered and violated the *temenos*. It is the wound of unbearable knowledge. In this not implausible origin myth for writing, it is a sacred wound, and poetry, certainly for C.P. Surendran, is an attempted suture for this sacred wound.

RANJIT HOSKOTE

NOTES

1. Telephonic conversation between C.P. Surendran and Ranjit Hoskote: 24 February 2016.
2. Telephonic conversation: 24 February 2016.
3. Ranjit Hoskote ed., *Dom Moraes: Selected Poems* (New Delhi: Penguin Modern Classics, 2012), p. lxi.
4. Ranjit Hoskote ed., *Reasons for Belonging: Fourteen Contemporary Indian Poets* (New Delhi: Penguin/Viking, 2002), pp. xxi-xxii.
5. Email exchange between C.P. Surendran and Ranjit Hoskote: June 2016.
6. Email exchange: June 2016.
7. Email exchange: June 2016.
8. C.P. Surendran, text message to Ranjit Hoskote: 9 May 2016.
9. Victor Klemperer, *The Language of the Third Reich: A Philologist's Notebook*, trans. Martin Brady (London/New York: Continuum, 2007), p. 14.
10. David Graeber in 'A Conversation between David Graeber and Michelle Kuo: Another World', in Maria Hlavajova and Ranjit Hoskote eds, *Future Publics (The Rest Can and Should Be Done by the People)* (Utrecht: BAK & Amsterdam: Valiz, 2005), p. 159.
11. James Agee, Preamble to James Agee and Walker Evans, *Let Us Now Praise Famous Men* (Boston: Houghton Mifflin, 1941), p. 11.

Riding the Horse of Life to Death: A Tribute

This is not a foreword. It was written as a tribute to poet Vijay Nambisan (1963-2017), and appeared in The Hindustan Times *a few hours after Vijay was no more. Why include this personal essay in this collection? Because, to my mind, it explains a way of writing and perhaps a way of living that characterized a few of us who began writing seriously in the early 1990s. I would venture to hope that should a reader like to read this collection sometime in the future, this essay might be helpful to her to call into reckoning a milieu. Besides I would like Vijay to be a part of this book.*

In the early 1990s in Bombay, poetry, or prose for that matter, was not about getting prizes. Or even being recognized in a bookshop or a restaurant. It was a defiant and dangerous personal vocation. Something like the helpless inner voice that urges a prospective Christ to climb his cross as a matter of course, and drive the first nail himself.

Poetry was a romantic, seemingly interminable act of self-sacrifice. First it required a measure of self-abuse. Then with luck words came. And they would sound real. For bad or worse, that has changed. Writing is a career now. A performance. A mime of the self. A frantic, if studied, method to hang on to what may not be there anytime now: an award, a fellowship, a flung nickel, an air ticket. And it involves one of the most tiring tasks an intelligent human can embark on: self-promotion.

Vijay Nambisan was capable of neither. In one of Vijay's prose works, *Language as an Ethic*, he argues from the heart—and shores up those arguments from his phenomenal intellect—that at the core of communication is not even words and images, but integrity. Devoid of it, language assumes a political and manipulative nature. On the surface of it, the premise sounds like the plea of an honest man to all to be good. But it explains, typical of Vijay's work, as in a flash, why a whole culture is incapable of facing up to truth at just about every level. And a people's proneness to collective delusions.

In the Bombay of the '90s there was a bunch of people from different generations who, more or less, spoke the then young Vijay's alien language: poetry. Dom Moraes, Arun Kolatkar, Adil Jussawalla, Nissim Ezekiel, Eunice De Souza, Jeet Thayil, to name a few. In my perception, at that time, among the senior poets Dom was closer to youngsters like us than the others. Dom was particularly encouraging of Jeet, Vijay, and me, regular visitors to Dom's residence in Sargent House, Allana Road, Colaba.

Dom had written, perhaps excessively kind, introductions and blurbs for the three of us, and recommended us to David Davidar, who published the now landmark Penguin Gemini series. As far as I can recall—and there is not much I am able to forget—most of us were on some mood-altering substance or the other most of the time, and had a certain contempt for what Vijay described as the Corporate Poet. And he did not mean just poet. He was against suits, boots, hats. And an equal measure of contempt for time; why else would we all try so desperately to fast-forward our clocks?

One of the accidental meeting points of the younger lot of poets was the *Debonair* magazine, whose office then was in Worli, housed in an unpretentious building. It would be always hot inside. And then there would be areas where it was wintry. The air conditioning was uneven. At the time, Anil Dharker was running it, and, like a classic liberal editor, he was open to new writers. The poetry editor for a while, if I recall correctly, was Imtiaz Dharker. The contribution of soft porn—recall the rose-filtered *Debonair* nudes—to English poetry has not yet been measured.

When Dharker quit, Adil Jussawalla took over. It was at this time that I first met Vijay. I had gone there, mid-morning, to follow up on an article, or perhaps admire a certain girl; Vijay was in Adil's cabin. He saw me and came out, grinning like he had met a cousin long lost. We went down to the bar round the corner and had a few. Sometime in the twilight hours, we parted, and all I could take away from that meeting was that I was supposed to meet him the next morning, at his paying-guest room close by.

I went, nursing the by now familiar hangover, and knocked on the door. Vijay opened it, but his face had undergone drastic restructuring. The night before he had fallen flat down the stairs on his chin, and was lighter for three or four teeth. There was blood on the stairs. I went back, in search of phantoms similar to Vijay so the imagined carnival could still take place; but could not find too many—even over the years.

I mention these details of the inner workings in the literary alleys of Bombay of that rather unchronicled writers' decade because Vijay stuck to that life, took several more falls. Lost more than his teeth.

The others moved on or tried to move from that unforgiving, transgressive life, in which words had to be bought with a little bit of life in exchange, an unsustainable trade.

Vijay bought into solitude, sometimes hating it, sometimes, choice-less, loving it. It gave him, I imagine, a martyr's identity. He was the knight of poetry, and he was going to ride the horse of life to death. The smarter among his friends veered away from that track.

Through it all, Vijay wrote. Not much, but a little that said a lot. For him it was hard to separate a way of living from a way of writing. To create, he had to destroy. And his own body seemed the closest at hand. At the centre of every poem, it seems to me, a bit of him lay bleeding ink.

He knew what he was doing. And, to me, it felt like a kind of vengeance. I was not sure vengeance against what. Most likely against himself. Between suicide and murder, he would choose the first. He knew his ways of life hurt people who loved him the most: his family; his very caring wife, Dr Kaveri Nambisan, a fine novelist herself.

A few times, he went off alcohol; but he unerringly came back to it, as he puts in a different context, in 'Reminders of Gain': 'The call of the arrow / Summons the bow.'

There are the usual articles doing the rounds that Vijay was a recluse. That word is a much-prostituted one in literary descriptions because it is used as if reclusion is a kind of extreme glamour of the eccentric. But then this is a place where the press described him as 'the first all India poetry champion in 1988'.

The truth was that Vijay was dysfunctional. The only place he could be himself and find a transcendental value was in the world of words. He was close to a few people. That kept shifting. For a while, or so I think, he was quite my comrade in arms; in alms, too: the early years in Bombay for instance. Then we drifted apart. In his later phase, he was perhaps close to Jeet.

In between, I moved to Pune to head the *Times of India*'s edition there. Vijay and Kaveri had taken up a house in Lonavla, where he said, the 'clouds passed through his head, if he opened the window.' I never did make it to Lonavla.

In the car from office to my house once, Vijay said, 'You have become a different man.' All the while I wondered how to tuck him in bed, given his slightly accusatory mood. Besides, in the morning we had to catch a flight to Bangalore, to visit a mutual friend who was going through a personal loss. I knew Vijay would drink through the night. He did not disappoint. At the airport the security said he had 'liquor on his breath' and that I would have to give a written undertaking for his safe passage. It occurred to me that Vijay turned himself into others' keeping without a second thought. He was naturally your responsibility.

This was around the time Vijay had done a rare, cadenced translation of selected portions of Poonthanam's *Jnana Paana*, (Song of Wisdom).

Poonthanam was a great sixteenth-century Brahmin Bhakti poet who more or less wrote the rules of the Malayalam language and literature. He was a devotee of Krishna, especially after the accidental death of his infant child.

Poonthanam's rival in Krishna bhakti was Melpathur Narayana Bhattathiri, a rather superior Brahmin—he was one of India's first astronomers, and he was a great mathematician and linguist as well—who wrote, *Narayaneeyam* in Sanskrit. Poonthanam's work made literature accessible to the non-Brahmin Malayalee. One of the great questions in Malayalam literature has been: Which work is better? Or which works better?

When Vijay said he was going to translate these ancient poets into English, I remember asking him, who's going to read it. We were at my place in Pune. Vijay asked for some salt. Because he sweated a lot, he would mix salt in alcohol. It was all quite scientific at one level. I got him salt. He blew some smoke in my direction and grinned his famous grin. He didn't care. That's what he meant. The market did not enter into the world of his words. His integrity was a voice that he could ever rely on to impel him to triumphs and disasters.

Later, he said the translation was no easy job. Though Vijay, like quite a few IIT-ians, had a photographic memory, he was not fluent in reading or writing Malayalam, even though he asserted his provenance and ethnicity wherever possible. What he did was to ask his father—who, when I met him once at his home in Bangalore, seemed both proud and worried about his prodigal son—for literal translations and then trans-created it beautifully into rhythmic wisdom.

Consider the opening lines of his work:

O yesterday the things we did not know would come!
And O the things we do not know will come today!
Now we behold those soon pass away!
We are not told how long they'll stay with us.

There is a touch of Hamlet here: 'There's a special providence in the fall of a sparrow. If it be now, 'tis not to come. If it be not to come, it will be now. If it be not now, yet it will come—the readiness is all.'

At the time when the book came out, it was mostly criticized for his self-confessed ignorance of the vernacular, and his own agnosticism. To my mind, it was a spectacular act of literary courage, though not easy to distinguish from self-indulgence, and cussedness.

Vijay drank. Went into detox. Came out. Wrote. Smoked. He smoked, I had often thought, as an antidote to alcohol. It was a break from what he was doing to his liver. For this, he had to destroy his throat and lungs. Either way, he would pay a price.

He paid it. Because the rest of the world of his '90s had changed. They had become gentrified. All the more reason he had to stay the course. He was the last man standing. He expressed what he thought of the change a few years ago in *Outlook*: 'Eighteen of the happiest months in my life were spent in rural Bihar. It may sound like reverse snobbery, but I can't help that. My wife and I were honoured members of the community, no one tried or wanted to shoot us, and the nuns looked after us like friends. What more could we want? A Learjet?'

This was the stay that went into the writing of his funny and insightful work: *Bihar Is in the Eye of the Beholder*. It explained, as perhaps only a poet could, the intricate workings of a place that failed to work, and still survived like a trick that explained the tawdry magic of India. This book too was commissioned by David Davidar of Penguin, with whom Vijay had a productive relationship.

That's saying a lot. Vijay's ties rose and ebbed with the tides of his mind. People betrayed him, by just not calling him up. In his mind, and I believe he was right, he was one of the few genuine artistes who deserved greater recognition, but would do nothing outside the covers of his books to wangle it.

His latest collection, which was released last year (2016), *First Infinities*, has some remarkable poems. It was perhaps justly brought out by an alternative publishing house, Hemant Diwate's Poetrywala. Some of the poems suffer from a certain vulnerability to fall into the rhymes and rhythms, which take the poet away from the place he intended to end up when he set out. But more often than not, the music ends in notes you did not think resided in them. It's only the fine permutation of the words that makes possible a beauty which was not there till Vijay thought it up:

> Snow
> Crisp in the winter's morning,
> Softly all through the night,
> What is this without warning,
> Falling and white?

I have never seen snow
But I can imagine it quite—
Not how it tastes, but I know
It falls and is white.
One morning I'll open the door
To bring in the morning's milk,
And all around there'll be snow—
Fallen and still.
How I'll roll in the stuff!
How I'll tumble and spin!
Until the neighbours cry, Enough!
And send me back in.

These are times when people die to live. Vijay lived to die. And write. I am glad I walked part of the way with him. He was the light. And he burnt furiously while he was there.

C.P. SURENDRAN
10 August 2017

From *Available Light*

A Note to the Self from Tranquebar

In a village by the noon, the sun rises in every room.
A shade of doubt, and I get the door. Vanakkam.
My father, brought to light by the sea. A petal I kept
To mark the pages of my life turns dark as the rum
Ove Gjedde took back to his silver mines in Kongsberg.

*

I try hard to add to the zero of my life without a sound.
In Tharangambadi, only the waves speak. Astride
A boat run aground, I watched the hot sea separate
Your thighs; from your crowned head, junk jewels of Janpath
Poured. Between breaths the earth keels over,
A million years to the minute. The sea.
The big, blue drawer of memory.

*

Where the long finger of water sleeps close to the sky,
A slow smoke of decay curls up like a dream.
Would that be a ghost ship drifting from Denmark to your hip?
Smoke meets wing. To an eagle, all that moves,
Moves towards its earth.
The Danes sold Dansborg Fort to the British,
Who, too, fled when the tide turned. Still the moon tugged
At the sea's heart. Still my father slaved through centuries of nights.
The beach flashes white and dark as the sea drags sunlight back.

*

At traffic lights, veiled women wail. Whips of blood
Split skin from songs. Drunks sight ships bulking
In empty air. Our ruins take shape as presidents
Wearing orange wigs. I uber; a cab my iPhone shook
Out of New York's brilliant dust; my head wrapped
In voices of David Bowie, Eminem,
The red-haired rest who overwhelm. The driver farts,

Hewn air, shaped like India, on the map. Shadows fall
Over the years, sunlight on soot. You eclipsed mirrors.
I made love to you everyday after you swam away.

*

I see my father at the door, bright as a beam
Of butterflies. Ghosts flit, like wind on water,
Everywhere in broad daylight. On my shoulder,
His hand; muscled in care, brown. I've taken it nowhere
Out of town, though I've dragged my feet through clouds of lead;
A moraine of sorts following my streets, like it was lost.
Where he touches burns, like a child on fire. When I arrive true,
The day before, or the day after, I must put my shoulder to the sea,
Watch it hiss; feel the waters part the heart like a passage to you.

Dolomedes Tenebrosus: Spontaneous Male Death

That May, summoned by screams, we went fishing.
Walked on water, blue as our blood, clear as a bell.
And I saw how you shot the finest silk from hell,
Mummy-shroud, from under your chevron feet,
The moon, and all that cried out captive to your spell.
Sucked on a soup of flesh, poisoned to perfection.
Your eyes shone like tiny lights in the nuptial night.
The world's webbed, and we're wedded—to our fate.

I tap and probe, eight legs courting eight of death,
The ballet of sex on a bed of leaves. We know how
This will end, all for good. My pedipalps enter you,
And inside you, the bulbs of future burn and break.
Spent, I cleave and cling to your loin: infant, and father;
And never was I closer to the beats of your heart.
Wrap me up in silk, your toxins my drip till my last.
Consume me end to end, egged-bitch, matriarch, mate.

Headcount

(2015. Towards the end of September, in Dadri, a village in Uttar Pradesh, about an hour's distance from Delhi, a group of Hindu fanatics battered fifty-year-old Mohammad Akhlaq to death, accusing him of dealing in beef. The violent after-effects continued for months. A year or so later, Akhlaq's son was beaten within an inch of his life for pressing charges.)

Mohammad,
On the nape of your neck
The morning cool like a knife's breath.

From Delhi's ruins,
September steps out in stealth
Like an assassin,
Tracks you down
Through the moving maze
Of every clock
To the precise hour of your death
In a lane no satellite can name.

The season's changing
Faint as the pall of ivy on stone.
Perhaps you have already seen it all.
The first red leaf foretells all of fall.

Stick out a finger to the wind.
Cattle and gods, kettle and drums
The caravan takes count, and finds
The day clear, loud, shorter by a head.

House Hunting

I open the door with a key shaped like a dagger
And sharp enough to pick its way through
The ribs, unlock the phantom-hoard of the heart.

I cross the hall and find the floor tilting
Towards the kitchen smoking like a pipe
After supper, the bananas yellow, and hooked,
Hanging from the roof by their stalks.

The washroom tiles preserve in dust
Little footprints like memory's fossils.
The study in which I'd breathe my last
As I closed a book is shorter by a chapter.

The balcony creeps into a wall of vines
That came away in my hands as I fell
When I was eight, and the air echoes
My knee's screams when its cap cracked.

I push against a door
I'd missed off the hall
Bracing to see my father bent
Over the desk, a fat green pen
Lit between his fingers,
Writing up a storm.

And see a boy in shorts instead,
Watching ink flow along lines that glow.
He looks up and says, welcome home.

Hadal

The waves white with what they witnessed
Below return, bowing and scraping
Along the shadows they throw
On shore; back,
Back to the silence thick as massed glass,
To first fish, time cutting teeth in the dark;
Ossified bones, hermaphrodite flesh, marine snow.

The cold is without thought. Things alive
Barely breathe. Your body sieves the sun
To the last. Here you are: in your element,
Feeding the sea out of your hand;
The memory-pumping heart is salt.

The sands rise from your pores,

There the shadows start.

Mirtaz, Daxid, Zapiz

Days narrow
Like the magic eye
Of an old radio.
Nights short
Like tweets.

At my window the creek climbs
With the sun and spreads
Over slush and sedge,
Merges with the day's white haze.

I take calls from users' club.
We discuss drugs
That breach
The blood-brain barrier,
Each guarded word
A coded cry for help.

Then it's night again,
Last light reddening
Receding waters
Revealing deep ruts, lanes.

I lie down hands clasped
Behind my head,
Listen to the blood
Flood and drain
Mind's shadow land.

Mirtaz, Daxid, Zapiz.

Journey

Wipes

At the airport, passengers move in order,
As if on a conveyer belt,
Watch their reflections gaze up at them
From the floor before transiting
To countries familiar and strange,
Their features slack with sleep lost
In transit; their faces are lined like maps,
Over which, a woman runs a rag
Carefully, as if to wipe away the jet lag.

Damage

On an old bag of mine, I count twenty-four tags,
Shades of blue, red and pink slips of paper, tied
To the straps and back, that show the distance
I travelled often between the same people;
A wedding, that droned on
Like a flight announcement,
Before it crashed; a death in the family
That brought everyone first to tears,
And then to blows; a divorce
That made the couple smile;
To people I learn to love always too late;
To books, to bars, to births and vast sunsets.
The tags on my bag flutter, tattered, torn; flags
Fading, like the passenger, with the passage.

Mask

Because of a bird, the grass rising steep on your left
Is the price we must pay for this flight.
When the cabin pressure falls,
The masks will drop on their own from the loft,
Pull them over your face, which keeps changing
Just like the skin that you shed
Once in four weeks completely.
Breathe deeply,
And let the scales fall from your eyes.

Omen

I make for the prayer room at the airport,
To thank the Lord for all he has done for me:
The tearless departures, the safe arrivals,
The unerring baggage claims, tepid tea.
The prayer room like my mind is white
As I expected, and I'm the only passenger

Who has taken pains to express gratitude
For the rewards that come from rectitude.
As I turn to go, a voice, clearly His,
Says, don't board this flight.
Why not, I ask, astounded,
Was it a mistake, did I hear it right?

The plane will land nose first, if you must know,
He says. Thank you, Lord, what about the others,
I ask him. They'll fly just fine, he says,
So long as you stay grounded.

Couple

At last she puts in a shy appearance
At the far end of the belt,
Having made sure the young,
Good-looking ones have left:
An old, bulging thing,
Last to leave a plane,
Waiting in places
From where people hurry to exit
For her ageing mate
Equally out of shape.

The pocket flaps are worn
To a thread.
The zippers are halfway down;
The mouth gapes
Like a sack undone.
One strap lags,
An arm that suffered a stroke.
The wheels drag.
Almost everything's more
Than she can contain.
I watch my bag go past me thrice
Before I take grip of her by the belly,
And we resume life, man and wife.

Signature

Gestures I trace to my mother
Her hands pick their aerial way
Through dire states of mind
The agonies of taking care
Of children who returned prodigally
From vocations. Her fingers
Are in curlers; they roll, preen
And part the air, knead a word
Into an abandon of tears. Forever
In motion, her hands have no limits
Nor remember the courtesy knock
Before a door is opened. Free hands
Flying farthest from gravity
Into high theatre where all words bow down
To the strung soliloquy of gestures
And the oracular act of nerves. Hands
That discern disasters balling up
Like storm clouds horizons away;
Whose certain coming she lets you know
By conjuring from sideboards
A crushed trail of broken glass.
Like the mute, my mother counts
The sinners and saints of the house
On her fingertips, the air around her
Bruised by signs of love.

Shakti Mills

The sun darkens stone.
The moon is a crazed,
Broken polygon.

A fissure in the earth
Reveals a cave
Emptied of
Reptilian death.

Here you went down
On your knees
Begging for a god-sent.

The night spreads
Its hood.
The sky brims with eyes.

Here you were taken,
Crushing grass
Grounding glass.

The wind gathered
Your rags,
Hung them on trees, bled.

Here you were born
Again and again.

The air kissed your face, fled.

Wordless

The somewhere-sea is here
Beyond belief; blue, deep as ink.

She falls at your feet again and again,
Having brought you to the brink.

Two

You shift in bed, next to me,
Your voice just right
For weather reports, blight.

'These are the words you like,
Dark, descend, stairs, nude, lantern, death
And you believe this is what your life is,
A few words, but perhaps not in that order.
Everything is richer than you think.'

I believe you are right.
Each life prints
Its dictionary;
Some a thesaurus
Of just one word.
What's yours?

I keep my peace
Aware of the sheath
Of space between us
Just right for a sword to hide
And worry why it takes
Just two people for such quiet.

Dhobi Ghat

Look back again
At the bodies labouring
By the black stream,
Their hands up to elbows slaked.

Over wet steps the sun foams
Like soap; these slathered slabs,
Flown in by time; milestones
From some laundered land.

One on which
My mother, too, sat, scrubbing linen,
In a courtyard noon-torched
Cursing loud at the mud-sport

Of those she wrung out from the dark
Into the clean day, and watch them pass
Body and soul, back into night as dust
Far from her hands, her face distraught.

Connected

End to end in August
The earth is breath
Rising
And falling
At the feat of wavering grass;
The violence
Whitening the stones
That sweat stories
Of the past.
You are here, or there.
End to end the meridian
Precise like a needle
Threads through us both.

Four Figures of Speech

Serial Killer

One in white on my right
Tells me what to drink,
Bright blood or wine.
I wake in the morning rain
And it's always the boy
Who hugs me tight
Whom I kill every night.

Voyage

I'm vague through strife.
I take orders from a woman in veil;
She wills rain between ships that sail.
I'm deathless in her arms and safe.
Her breath is cold as mist.
We sleepwalk through waves of wrecks
Towards what was there on the decks.

Steam

You came whistling at the window
The day after your daughter died.
We cut with fingers on the pane
Figures of ghosts. We froze white
When we saw her wave from the shrubs.
Our kiss blew her out of sight.

Unborn

Your curls for the curdling clouds
Your smile for the dawn's first milk.
There's a rose high over thorns, it's yours.
You come, you go. And I'm to blame.
You never went, you never came.

Retro

You walk into neon-walls of the night
Wearing the same glasses that dimmed
Your morning. The city has aged out of sight.

You run into women talking of their prime,
Rolling glasses on foreheads
To straighten the wrinkles of time.

The streets are blind; the beggars mellow
Outside cafes of a kind. The band plays songs
Black and white. The last kiss tastes like the end.

It's almost the same city; just that everybody's
A little slow, fat. The morning rain's thin
As your hair. The mirror drives the cab in reverse,
All objects farther than they appear.

The End of an Affair

The wind reads water well,
Ripple and swell;
Spreads your hair like a veil
Over the moon.
Your promises,
Like secrets,
Are not kept;
The night, spotted
With stars, crouches,
Like a leopard
Before it leapt.

Installation

Today I put up my house for sale,
Clearing all the furniture except
The writing desk.
They went up a truck,
The six-drawer dresser with mirror
In excellent condition
Staring at me all the way,
And turned the corner.

I drove around
Just looking at things
In the rain,
Sat on a bench in a park.
I got back late, wet.
I took my jeans off
And placed it over the desk, legs hanging
Loose as if they were broken at knee, the hips
Collapsed to coccyx, the belt snaking around
A stomach shaped like a giant pear
Opening up at one end.
The whole thing looked like a man waist down
Spread-eagled, stone-drunk,
Except that I was sitting in a corner
Naked, watching him go to bed.

Marxists

I had gone in and taken my clothes off before I fell in bed
When I realized the bio of Eleanor Marx was on the sofa.
I braved the cold in my briefs and retrieved the book
To read myself to sleep and wake, resurgent,
In honour of the working poor.

Then it was my glasses, which caught me stark naked.
I was fishing for them under the table in the hall
When the door opened and my neighbour came in
In a slip, asking for a book, and wearing my glasses,
Looking like Rosa Luxemburg.

We groped our way back, hand in hand,
And equitably shared Eleanor Marx on the rug.

Engagement

A ring of cloud
Slipping down
The finger
Of a cliff.

What the Doctor Said

Don't drink
When you are on Mirtaz,
Daxid, and Zapiz.
Because you'll see vultures
Perched on the window
Or strut in through the door.

I stayed with that for a while,
And away from ink.
But when the rain got too much
And I flipped
Through the album
Of the dead in my head,
Their eyes full of life
And their being nowhere in sight,
Moved me to drink.

I returned late and fumbled,
Wondered if this was a key without a lock.
At long last, all of it came away in my hands
Lock, stock and barrel, and though I was drunk
And sweating like beer in the sun
I could see in the dark
All their faces luminous like lamps.

Cowboy

These roads are good now,
Clean, deserted,
Fit to walk, or stage a duel.
A lone Victoria, slow,
As if the horse was drawing
The whole city after it,
Is the only traffic.

The lamps on Marine Drive burn,
Like candles to the blind;
The footpath is salted
With spray;
The parapet taciturn
But for a couple split
By a wedge of sea
Gazing at Arabia
Where the sands must shift.

In a clock full of 4 a.m.-s
This would be the city to live in
And write a song; perhaps end an affair,
If only, amigo, bleeding, you could trust
A horse to take you home.

Mirrors

When we are done with the nature of light,
At what great speed it travels, the evil it does
To mass; its tricks with the eye,
Refraction and reflection, finally
We are left with time.

When a child, I could see
In the glass on the wall
A lot of my forehead.
Later, only the chin,
As my grandmother was short.
There have been other mirrors
When all my features
Came to light, and yet I had lost
My face, and I had begun to look
Like my ancients, a forefather there,
An uncle here, all having travelled
By rays of light into the great hall of glass.

These magisterial dead stare at you from afar,
Distances measured in irreversible events,
Till you give in and blink,
And mirrors within mirrors,
They all go blank;
That's the time to cross over, turn,
Full eye and no mercy, return
The favour to the next in line.

Justice

You've reappeared in Rambo gear.
They gave you the job that cost us dear.

Don't do it, I said, feeling like a mess;
You're old; besides they buck-shot Tess.

There's more to do of the same, you said.
Now that I'm risen like the sun, all's red.

I tell him then the name of the game
New rules; but guns, he says, are the same.

My father rides the escalator like a king:
The dead return trained in everything.

Defiance

These chairs stuffed, welcoming with arms open,
Head-cushions, and leg rests, are thrones fit for a Herod.
At thumb, a button draws you level with the ground,
Once used for burial, then a dumping site, now a mall
Housing a salon for those who believe appearances
Will win the round; close shaved and hair trimmed,
They flee through mirrors their skin, risking all
To fall in line as he comes, smelling the compliance
Of shampoo, tonic, powder and cream, and sprinkles
Water on your head as if to douse a fire.
You close your eyes to the hair swept to a corner,
Flecked with blood, and wait for the blade to bite
As with hands that might hold down a calf,
He presses a razor to your throat, and you think of John
Staring at Salome from a plate, his locks still dread.

Repeat Radio

A radio comes on in my head, one with six valves; slow,
Like a petro-lamp, to light up; two knobs that turn the world
On its head before sound issues, and a cockroach transfixed
At Madras, its antennae moving as if to fend off noises
Gregor Samsa might have heard in his head.

I play it by ear. The insect is sound of health;
His eyes alert like the ones I've seen in the head
Of a soldier, witness to his friends falling at sunrise.

Last night, for a moment I took my eyes off the bug.
From Madras the news broke,
Things are no longer the same.

When I looked again,
He was gone without a trace,
And I stood beneath the needle in his place.

Absolute

When will you let her go?
If I bring the cash in hand
Will you let her go?
If I mail you my ear
Will you let her go?
If I stared at the sun till it turned to coal
Will you let her go?
If I brought my two rooms in a box
Will you let her go?
If I sold all my books for a little gold
Will you let her go?
If I walk, on all fours, a hat on my ass,
Will you let her go?
If I send my son
Who smiles when it rains
Will you let her go?
If I rip my head and shred it like bread
Will you let her go?
Tell me what'll it take to let her go?
Tell me why you won't let her go?

Tell me whoever you are, you fucking so and so.

Prophecy

Memories, she contended,
Are the brick and mortar
Of ruins; and that's how
The evening ended.

Hoopster

Son, you can't go wrong,
A Michael Jordan
Of life's longest loops,
All your body aligned
At last to the arrogant crown,
To shoot your head bang
Into the ring of thorn.

Graveyard Shift

Self-recrimination

The things in my head lead me round the corner
To the cemetery, where the dead make a point
Of silence. I walk about a little and, soon, call it quits:
The fittest man must have mud thrown in his face.

I lie down on the earth, home to someone
Freshly arrived, his tombstone for a pillow,
The leaves whispering
A wreath around my head,
And watch time toss torches
Through the trees,
A passage lit for autumn's drift:
Some leaves decaying to gold
And some red like a melon split.

Deep in the pit, the worms circle the sun
Worrying those who took the final steps
Away from light and found a shift
At rest, working blind to their finger tips
For those left gazing at autumn on earth.

Lodi Garden, Winter

What can one say of Sikander Lodi
But that he ruled Delhi for 28 years
Had many more women,
Fathered Ibrahim,
Razed temples, built mosques, killed for fun,
And like any other thing, died (1527), though a king.

His tomb sprawls over the garden, an empire
Of ruins; how in death Sikander has grown,
A vast corpse worth his weight in stone.

The evening is red as befits a lord whose word
Was as good as his sword, a long steel tongue,
Dipped in blood, and independent of head.

From where I stand, I see a blade cut
The sun in two, the first stars paling
At the scimitar art. King or thing,
Tonight I'll drink to stone and grass.

―――

Monotony in NY

Far below, the cars stretch
Like limos into coffins.
I climb on to the window,
Dregs of a drink in hand,
A routine trick
I perfect night by night,
And wonder which
Make to choose:
The one in the centre
Snow-wreathed,
Or one by the side,
Fat and big
A rich man's pride.

There are more choices down there
Than meet the eye
If only I lean out
A little into the wind,
A current crazing the body
And the fall would be free.
And if, on the way down, I drained
The glass like a rake
I could be on a high
When I land
And lead my wake.

Conversation with a Nine-Year-Old on God, Devil, and Life after Death

Q: Do you believe in god?
A: Yes, of course. He's there.
Q: Where?
A: Up there.
Q: Why not down?
A: He likes to fly.
Q: Devil?
A: He exists too.
Q: A proper devil?
A: He is made of concrete. Wears sunglasses.
Q: And god?
A: He is made of soul.
Q: What's soul?
A: It's a child. It doesn't grow.
Q: Is there life after death?
A: Yes, we are living it

Erasure

Drain

'I remember the way you forced your brush
Against your teeth, cleaning the last of the leftover words.
Aggressive. I stood by the door and watched.'

Yet, when you faded from the pool of glass
And my face was clear in it
I brought up the whiskey,
Coffee, and bile
Into the zinc
And a little bit of rusted metal
That chinked against the drain,
A piece of the armoured heart.

Water Colour

You walk on the shadow
That the sun spreads
Like a carpet on the steps
Leading up to the great paintings
Framed in time.

Woman ascending stairs,
You gather your skirt about you,
Smile into the camera
In the hands of a passing Swiss,
Who flew over the Alps
To cross your path just in time.

Years after we parted, I chanced on this snap
In a drawer crammed with reprints
Of the Masters. Your face had yellowed,
Like a paper curling inward in fire,
And your lips were dipped in blueberry jam.
That was cancer easing me out
Of frame, you texted,
A week before they lowered you into October slime.
And though you had done me a wrong back there,
I thought time had too soon committed a crime.

Passage

This may sound complicated like clockwork
Or simple as the chimes struck
By hours that are no more. There was a train
Issuing out of the night; it bore us into the day
Broadening the city into vision, where we'd stay:
Two characters in our own grim fairy tales.
We lived them true to their last word in this city,
And their echoes ring in my ears long after you've left
Faint and mysterious as sounds from infinity.

Third Person Singular

The people we met as a couple at parties
Workplace, pubs, and bickering homes
Grow solemn at the news come to them late
And stare at me as if I had a hand in the crime.

We talk about you as if you were someone else,
Your sharp takes, humour, the way you crinkled
Your nose at mischief, a feat beyond those who left
This light, before we move on to the weather.
And everything about you that we recall
In such detail, a stranger reintroduced by death
To earth, confirms you were invisible when alive.

———

Memorabilia

A murder of crows
Cry out the miracle of the day.
A chopperful of flies descend
From heaven, kissing their seats
Clean in honour of their arse.
Termites bear away the roof to supper.
Far below in the haze of rain
Cars scream like babies in pain.
I toss in bed, too broad for one,
And think of the stones we made skip
And bounce on a stream issuing
Long ago out of a naked noon.

———

Incest

And those days before the mall.
The man at the shop said, when I asked
For noodles, your sister came and got it.
The next day, it was the brother buying

Bread and butter ahead of you
By an hour or two in the rain.
It's the way we walk, you said, hands on
Each other's shoulder, though that wasn't how
We slept. Incest is best, you said,
When our parents are not wed.

———

Disconnection

Tonight they came and cut power
For reasons of repair, and what does
Forgetfulness entail but the dark?
I go about the house and find the furniture
Out of place. How dead things move
Us to trip and cry? I sit on the floor,
And switch on the cell to see
In out-worldly light
A missed call from what was once
Your number,
Which if I return must surprise
A face belonging to another place.

———

Solo

Wingspan of the sky
Measured
By wing beats
Of a sparrow.

———

Mismatch

It wasn't all good while it lasted.
But that was all I had,
Though it wasn't love, it was close,
Something like my hand in your glove.
You trailed a bare finger on the frosted glass,
As we drove up the mountain.

Nothing remains
Of those days, those mountains
Floating like icebergs stripped
Of ocean,
Not even a snap, except this image
Of your signing off:

Notes of a music
Only you've heard,
Shoved deep into a pocket
Of my mind.

They spill and slide into view

As I bend and slip a foot into the wrong shoe.

―――

Last Supper

A mushroom pie for me. Ice cream for you
That would last for ever.
I look at you, terminal patient
In a cafe full of laughter, hoping you wouldn't notice
The glint of guilt in my eyes. Your hair is matted;
There is still no grey in it. No silver lining,
You said, though I can see

Patches of scalp, like clearings in the grass.
Your gums are black. Your body bloated,
Soft, like bread soaked in water.
And you are covered
In stonework that clunked when you moved.
I'm immensely wealthy, you said,
As you paid the cheque,
And don't I look as if I'm in my prime?

And a week later I realize,
You never touched the sweet,
And the little on your card
Was enough to last your life.

Morning Glory

Eyes prise open dawn,
A grey ray of light under the door
Reaching out to touch the feathers
Of a dead dove. It was not war gathering
Its drums as I imagined in my sleep,
But the bird trying to wing its way out
Into the freeways of the night,
Past the far milestones of stars.

A Promise in South Sudan

Here they come, lean, hungry, and all under twenty
With sticks, spears, and guns poking the sky
As if to see if there is some life left up there.
Boys who grew up too fast, and left home,
Silently swearing to their mothers,
They will remain young
And beautiful forever, their eyes empty, and yellow
With the gold of the desert sun they fight for and die.

S.O.S

'Hello, and sorry, every time you called I was busy or travelling.
It's been crazy. All well with you?'

I think I made calls to you, but the signals
Here are weak. And the time zones.
Since the whole Atlantic deepens
Between us, the sun would be shining
In your world,
While mine would be dark, naturally.

Yes, I'm good, thank you, but when I think...

You would've been busy, of course,
The day's demands are telling on all of us.
In any case, I call for nothing, really; last night
It was because of the way the creek shimmered
Yellow in the full moon,
And the far hills lay submerged
Like elephants bathing.

Is that a reason? Is there a reason?

And is there a possibility of us meeting,
Far in the future, no doubt?
We can look out on the water
At the evening coming over?
This might sound a little strange,
But do try to message me before you call,
An alert, that's all.
As I said, here, I'm mostly out of range.

Phantoms

Reflection

There was the sight when I caught a bus late one night
Of a man driving a pin up the heel of a baby bawling
In the arms of his mother. I got out with him
At Harbor Terminus where trips turned around.

What makes you do that, I asked?

Oh, my friend, he said, I train spoilt babies
To grow up tough, so they take the world
In their stride, and hopes of the mothers
Are not belied. I'm sure you took your first steps
On shattered glass. It shows. Be my guest,
Come and have a drink at home.

Some other time, I said, and I was afraid
It might all turn out to be wrong.

He smiled: I, too, took my time
To find my trade. Come again, same bus,
And let's set it right; at night we see it all
In a different light.

On the far sea I saw a ship docked
Between two stars, shedding and loading
Its cargo of fireflies. From darkened homes
I heard babies wailing through the night.

Bender

The Member of Parliament is an affable man.
He has a face like kneaded dough, and two dark holes
With a little bit of water in them for eyes.
He called me over home for dinner
But I couldn't make it because the trees were turning
Black, and everything was drawn in charcoal
Against an orange storm.

Last week, I found myself near his place, and rang the bell.
Someone like him wearing a long skirt, lipstick and mascara
Opened the door and said, Do I know you?

No, I said, because one heart could pump blood for two.

———

The Departed

When I was a child, and up to no good
An Armenian on a battered bike and out of place
In Madras sold my father the Book of Knowledge;
All nine volumes grey as his leathery face
So he could catch a flight home from his lodge.

In less than a year the shelf was lined with books,
Which my father bought to make me bright,
And perhaps paid the lion's share of Gregory's fare.

Because no one else bought a line in that brilliant town
Gregory drank through day and night, missed his flights,
And one day, farthest from his home, died in his room,
Shrunk by half in his coat in the famous Madras glare.

Cleaning the shelves tonight, I took the volumes down,
And came upon this photograph, fading brown:
My father and Gregory on the bike, staring
At their ward, not a word wiser for all he read.

Spooked

I see them all the time, men and women
Lit by the sun, greeting each other
With a smile or a wave of the hand,
Or, walking across foyers, faces split
In the glass, in trousers and skirts,
Often coffee in hand,
And executing similar acts
Of extreme nonchalance.

It is as if they haven't travelled
Perched as dust
On a rock
Blasted off
From a distant star.
As if the sky will not fall;
That the earth will not shake its rivers off.
And at night, the heavens shining just right
Over where they got off
A while ago
Without a thought.
Spirits then, but for the flesh,
And faint and fleeting,

As breath on glass.

Apocalypse

There is nothing today, not one word, not a sound,
Not even an image except at one backward glance,
This long room, with a table and a bench,
And a mattress on the floor to one side, expectant.

If one day, they laboured
Brick by brick, and extended this place
Over the creek to the horizon, they'd find me on edge
Dangling my feet in air over the same window ledge.

Weather—and Other—Reports

The knock on the door, followed by the thwack of something
Dropping dead on the floor, is what man did to man or dog,
In black and white and all the shades in between, so you know
An old war is drawing fresh blood in your neighbourhood,
That your lover has changed her gender after much pain
And has now become like you, hard, unforgiving, regretting
Everything. Someone in a village up north, where the snow
Is feathers that a bird shakes free to see if its body is black,
Has shot the bridegroom leaning from the terrace, out of joy;
He was, the report adds, aiming at the sky. The poor are
Better off, the old are living longer. Pythons have become
Popular as pets. So it goes. You look out of the window,
See in the east a needle probing the skin of water,
As if for a vein, the creek's first fix of light.
You can begin your day, or end it; the sun goes down
Like a trick, according to the Met, sharp at 6:36.

False

Tonight I'm a little drunk, I admit, but I can drive
My way back home, make my bed, pull in corners
All correct, perhaps lie down in my jeans, straight
As, say, my father in state, or a friend who thought,
Falsely, it turned out, symmetry pre-empted suicide,
Thinking how the night shines, and wish
They all came back to life like light
And we spoke on how we might have been kinder
To each other though I wouldn't want
Them to linger on for too long because, given a chance,
We tend to regress to the first person,
Which explains why I, autodidact, had a problem
With them when they were lit bright by a younger moon
And, dazzled, I'd prayed for a cloud to dim the sight.

Diadem

My friend the failed actor is suffering from migraine.
He suspects, naturally, cancer, or some such malady
Is on its way, since his last play in which he was Christ
On the cross, soliloquizing on betrayal and belief;
But the thieves by his side moved the audience more.

The director resurrected a substitute on the third day,
And Christ was asked to go home, far from stage, to Mary,
His mother. Ever since, he said, I have this ring of pain
Going around my head like a crown of thorns.

Umbilical Cord

This windshield presents
A three-year-old girl
On a fraying rope,
A stick in hand to steer her course,
Through the monsoon clouds, and hope.

On earth, her father beats a drum,
A one-man tribe sending out sounds
Of distress, wishing he was drunk,
So he could stop feeling like a bum.

The lean one in long skirt, the end of the rope
Passing through the stakes and tied to her waist,
Is the mother looking up at her child
Learning to walk with such sure steps so soon
After birth the silver line between life and death.

Pawn

How serendipitous to reach by cut and thrust
Through rival ranks, to that distant hall,
A refuge from the avalanche of nights and days,
Watch, as a child with eyes wide, the bright dreams
Framed and hanging like lanterns from the wall,
Walk along the chequered squares of the floor,
Past rooks painted blue, and bishops carved
In wood, buttressing the roof, lost gambits,
Towards the king, to my father's bed, warm
Like a remembered hug, and lie awake at first light,
One leg trailing on the floor, the other on the blanket,
To the heart beating in memoriam, half in, half out of time.

Still Life

The long room is silent like oranges in a basket,
And smells of formaldehyde. Is it the bright fruit
Going off on a table in the far corner?
Through a window in the coved ceiling sunlight drips
Like rain. The walls are covered in red silk damask,
As befitting the long life that shed tears
Whenever lovers bled to death, swords buried
Deep in the graveyard of their hearts.
Eighty-eight black-and-white portraits of the star,
Long before she dissolved out of sight,
Hang from the wall,
Like postcards from a time
When the world was a hall of fame,
And flashbulbs popped from every eye,
And there she may have stayed, sylph for ever.

Now she sits, on something like a throne,
Inside a box of glass for fear of air,
Wearing someone's hair; her face,
A battleground of brushwork
Before mirrors sworn over fire
To secrecy; a painted mask of youth
Through which ancient eyes dare
You to spot a flaw in her past,
The barely breathing
Present object of art notwithstanding.

Umbrellas in Hong Kong

(*On the public protests in 2014*)

A light portable cover for protection from rain or sun
Consisting of a fabric held on a collapsible frame, say,
Of thin ribs radiating from the top of a carrying stalk
Can also, like a hundred flowers, bloom in the air
When Xi's gardeners arrive with guns and pepper spray.

Sparrows

In Gaza, Kobane, Kashmir
There is a moment of hush,
In retrospect,
Before a bomb explodes
And the air begins to bleed.
This is the time no clock marks
Because hearts are about to stop.

When it goes off, sound and light
Separate, like a sieve, mother and child;
Human innards trail on the road,
And festoon the branches
Like badges pinned to military green.
The clamours of those yet breathing
Mingle with screams out of sight;
Nightmares haul the day after them
And the high-voltage evening rusts
And sparkles along the razor wires.

Some will gather their last breath
To ask what happened to passers-by.
Others will think of their children
Left to wander the earth looking
For what they lost
Till they met death eye to eye.
And, cruelly, no one remembers the enemy,
Or whose turn it's next; from whose chest
Flesh will fly like sparrows from a nest.

Day

Sickness is the closest we came to old age when young,
And we went to bed after milk to escape the ills
Of the day, into the prophylactic dark, lit at its heart
By the imagination's countless lamps,
Where all logic is wish,
And woke, unable to lift an arm,
Or turn our heads to see the haze shimmering
Like lace from the window, or to just breathe
Because a cold had stuffed the nose with phlegm
And we thought the end was upon us
Before we got old and wise like the rest of them.

Night

From the heart of rain an eagle drops
Like a ball of lead, wet wings folded,
A lethal prayer whose answer
Is the beak buried in some furry neck:
A twitch in the flesh of time,
And the sun scratched out from its eyes.

*

All my past turns me into stone, a Midas,
Someone shouts in the dark, of misdeeds.
I can barely recall the acts,
I'm laid on my back, on horses carved
Out of the block of the night,
Two stiff parts joined by a bitten bone,
And if I straighten I will crack like scone.

*

'Rat or roach, we all dine on each other,
An extreme art we take to our grave.
And here, my friend, is a bucket of cocks
Skinned. Those were figures that braved
Speech once. You see the pain here?
It's only just that you pay, this is the mart,'
The curator tells me from behind her veil.

*

I notice a naked bird perched on her shoulder,
Its wings plucked; it drinks from her clavicle.

*

The curator pauses, head to one side,
As if to listen to the vein ticking
In my neck, a jugular trick,
That keeps me alive, and says:
'At midnight I set sail,
And everything must go before
I go; on board, I hope to take the veil off
And bare my bones to the stars.
At sea, I'm free.'

*

I wish I could see your face, I tell her,
But some vague thought has caught
My voice mid-throat.
I can only stare at the rain,
Falling into my eyes.
What moved me to this?

*

The night grows wings, bangs its blind head
Against the walls. Or is it the hooves running
Circles in my head? Once there was a world
And horses were its measure, the moon its torch.

*

And all night you read my palm wrong.

*

The walls are lit by dreams, framed and hung
By some famous hand that surely knew the song.
Such silence. I can hear a pulley creaking
Over a dry well. That'd be hope. My head's turning
Through sleep to green stone, the moss creeping
Up from my toes, a blanket death draws up with care.

*

If my pillow is wet, I can't tell tears from blood.

Double Decker

As dreams come, this was without a heart as any,
And I have seen, just like you, so many. If I cut the details,
When I sneezed, the snot landed on an Austrian blonde,
A green scar on her pink arm, and she screamed.

What's a stage actress doing, steering a bus in and out
Of the city's narrow streets when it was neither light
Nor night? An ashen haze shrouded the towers
And the ghettos as Bombay, like a specter,
Emerged from the shredded muslin of wet October.

Nothing I read or wrote could undo my act,
Or clean her arm. I watched her go up the stairs
And disappear like a dream.
I took the driver's seat, but the wheel was in her hands,
And she was on top.

In this manner my marriage came to a stop.

The Plain of Jars

(To Fred Branfman, exposer of America's secret war in Laos, who died on 24 September 2014)

'I felt that although I might have to die, it did not matter; that I just had to be happy in the midst of all the sadness of war, of the airplanes dropping bombs.'

All through the night I heard someone cry.
It was not me, it was not a dream, but as I lay in bed
And watched a plane cross the midnight sky,
I knew it wasn't a lie.
Right now a gun's being fired, a woman raped,
A child orphaned, a man between knives
Is on his knees, and a field goes up in flames.
All's changed, all remain the same,
It'd be morning soon, and it might rain any time.

There Was a Man in the Land of Uz

I

Lord, here I am, short and dark, with a substance
That will not take me far, and a car worth now
Not a she ass. But I have been faithful to you
As only a drunk can towards distant light
Though the path wavers day and night,
Those black-and-white postcards you
Deliver dire to the doorstep,
You messenger leopard, you.

Invisibly inked, your writs are mysteries,
Unravelled by the sun and, as often the moon, mostly sad
As infants who never saw light; the cruelty of it all
Pointless as a bomb dropped in an anatine pond,
Numbing as the mother sundered from her child,
No matter what Eliphaz, Bildad or Zophar try
To say in your praise and win your case.

Your babbles are accurate as dust
In the beginning,
Their significance clear afterwards
Like a car crash; genesis of tragedies lit up
In the ghost light from a dead star,
The details precise when blood's spilt?
All is clear when all is done.
I am confounded because of hope:
How explain a shock of corn in its season,
Before an ill wind scatters it?

II

Bildad was at the wheel showing me a way
When he plowed my car over the divider;
Trust in god, he gasped, as if his last breath
Was ballast for another war that I must fight.
Eliphaz and Zophar were in the back, and they fled
As humans do when they are face to face with dread.

Figuring out your wishes, I sneezed for long
Allergic to the air I breathe. For me it wasn't oxygen
You meant? On the windshield you played origami
With my good friend's blood. And I see his teeth are long
As seeds of fig, and that his heart is in his mouth.

I crawled out through the window, a dumb thing
Decorated with the metal of my mangled fate,
On to the road, my mind broken like a bow.
Bildad you sowed, Bildad you reaped.
The band of his bones you drew out from his flesh.
You snuff out lives before a moth,
And the insect too dies before he is wise.

III

How explain your will?
The mountain of anger you move
To block our path,
And headlong we crash.
Or is this too pride,
These questions I ask on all fours
Under the sky,
Whose holes brim with tears of my wrath.

IV

It has been one long night.
In the east I see a glimmer.
The dark, fractured,
Bares a bone;
Or is it you finally opening your eye a crack?
You see me sitting in the dark
Between the street lamps
Head in my arms;

And the first dust must rise
And sing in your ears
Sweet as psalms.

Grace: Woman Metalling Road

Where she sits on her haunches the sea fell away
Fifty million years ago, baring the mountains.
The dirt track leads through
Clouds, shines mineral white,
Travels to the enemies of her country
And her gods.
A truck trundles close to the edge
Of everything, men in fatigues with guns
Across laps, stare at clocks on far family walls.
On a bed of cardboard and sackcloth
This close to heaven, a baby bawls, face red
In protest. His mother chisels bread
From her day's granted stones.

An Act in November

The sun finds a way
Around the courtyard
Twenty floors below.
Pigeons flock on shadows
Dark as water on sand.
You toss a fig, a filament
In the making since first light,
A sign from the skies
For birds to break into flight.

The day brightens with applause.

As Kill a King

The wrecking of your bed.
Who lay here warming the teak but you,
And my mother years ago when I fled
Towards my fate.

At the cross-roads between dreams
And memory, amber and red glow lights
Of eternity. There I killed the king,

Blind before and after.

David, Don't Be Sad, That Was a Dream

Selection

Dawn rusts the barbs,
Sheaf of words,
Sheath and sword,
Melts snow red.
You sleep on a cow's lunch
Under a sky in convulsions
Of black and white
Between the wings
Of crematorium crows.

In the trench, where the wind stammered;
A few breathed still, their oxen jaws open,
And three worked with bayonets
Gutting a horse.

*

In thinning rows
Of five, or four, they count;
Left and right,
We march, and our heads fall
To zebra-days like blows.

Your son swells the tide,
He is naked this winter; body
Pale like light drowning in the deep.
There is no space for grass
Between the boots that grow.
All you held to heart is
Smoke.

We have come to a place
Of the past,
The wasted drift of yellow stars.
You are a stone
Come to life muttering Kaddish.

*

And you rise from the grave
Of those days, Alles heraus,
Again and again
To commands dropping dead
Against the door.
You light the stove
The air blue
Like poison's tongue.

And you recall you never had a son
Nor cursed your mother with a wife;
Far or near the days of strife,
You're lucky to die alone
Every day like the sun.

Kristallnacht

You stayed on the mat
Long after the moon
Filling the skylight
Dragged its veil of gold
Over the night's dead,
The fires in hell stoked
By a god fat as bread.

In the kitchen,
The woman wearing clogs,
In whose eyes winter wept
Whose promise you sensed
In the thick of dying breaths,
But was not, after all, kept,
With whom upright you slept
As the Shabbat spun the world
A shroud.

Abandoned the stars.
Abandoned the children.
Roots break
Away from branches,
The leaves are white.
Abandoned
The synagogue
Of Zerrennerstrasse.

Here she comes
Through those stolen days
Of butterflies,
Eyes shut,
Hands cradling the baby
Praying for your grace
As if you were a Kapo
Or a king.

You writhe between betrayal and belief,
Yours is the chosen race, but not for praise,
Thinking of the last of your children and wife
Caged in their bones, as centuries shake and fall
Like pebbles in a tossed tin,
Each separated from each
By the same stripes
Laid like lashes on the skin.

On their shoulders sprout wings of snow
Scarecrows stripped for final flight.
You hand her a toothbrush
Salvaged from the dark
And hope she makes it,
Far from where the dead
Continue to burn,
Towards heroic spaces
Where epic potatoes blaze.
She screams, Aufstehen,
Epitaph to a million men
Barefoot and naked
On the long road
That ended
At the narrow gates
Of the Lord.

*

Christ hangs by his nails from the wall.
You sit up and watch the flies
Circling your head
Like a crown
And smile at last
Having survived
Another night
Of broken glass.

Witness

Grow white in the pit of skulls,
Hair far removed from head.
Walls are alive; they draw
Features of those who've gone.
Penitent alder, beech and pine
Confess snow red as wine.
Bare feet march and bow
In step
With fate's crooked line.
Equal the dreams of the dead.
We were many
And the time was short
Tread your way through grass,
Staring out of eyes,
Lifting their head
Long after gales
of high boots pass.

———

Regiment

Here are so many mouths
Lying
Far from face.
And one must belong
To you
And to young Eliahu
Brave in all his breath;
Or someone else.

C.P. SURENDRAN

It's hard to tell
One from the rest
In this blood-red light
When they are
Equally bereft of earth.

Once Upon a Time

Moon forged
In the remote fog of future

The sea splutters bodies
Lowered like lanterns.
The flags are forgotten;
Those barks, too,
More than a language,
A manner
Of laughing, almost.

In silence, we plumb our own depths
Down to starlit bottom
Surprised as night birds
By light.

Vein

Down the shaft of sleep
Foul ore of open mouths
Wrench from lips
Grimace
Twisted like pliers.

Extract gold,
Hidden deep like filling,
From such things as smiles.

———

Lingua Tertii Imperii

The night at the edge of knife
Extends remembrance endlessly.
How they ran round and round
In enormous shoes
Of thorn, how they looked forever
For the ice of what's gone;
How the earth shook
Under thrones;
How a bullet emptied
Them of the earth.
How from helmets grass sprung
Again in innocence of pain.
How language,
Leashed to that place and time,
Barked and growled,
And Cerberus understood.

———

Boy Who Saw No Tree, Bird, Star

Heart's dark
Splits to spew out
A tiny arm
With a tattooed number,

Hurbinek, paralyzed waist down,
Son of man.
His mother ascended
The air
Silent as smoke.
He fought
From the day of his birth
To enter the world of men,
Was moved
From bunker to bunker in stealth
And in three years
Reached
The end of earth.

———

The Twilight of the Gods

White winds drive up the slopes of night,
Like porters bent, trees, under sacks of leaves.
Beneath unbroken skin,
Ice-lands hold fast.
This music is ichor
Turned from gold
To midnight blue,
Each note
Struck like the final hour of the dark.
What image drowns in unseeing eyes?
Hidden in the loft,
Who stokes and sets the sky,
Its far legions on fire?
What cities burn on tongue
What houses fall

And cover the streets
As thunder shakes the clouds?
What fated future brings the past to the fore?
What bent ray of light pierces heart's core?

―――

Jukebox in Colaba

Hammer this day into your heart
Step out into the unearthly place
Milling with unjustified absences,
Spinning children worn to the skin
Around the sun;
Make pain anew, like Christ.
They press their lips, a scar, stamped on the glass
Of stranded cars; the junkies sleepwalk
The collapsed bridges in pools of piss.
The gents in their suits
Empty like tins
In the gentle rain.

The cattle with their painted horns accuse
You from the back of a truck.
Near Café Mondegar, they let the tailboard down
And you wondered if the sky was drunk.
Listen, as if drawn to a vice:
They are playing Mamma Son Tanto Felice;
Time to dance on the ashes.
Your steps are slow.
Your eyes are soot.
You grind your friends underfoot.

Washing

Black, some nearly blue as ink,
Ashen, gold, even red,
Spread out on the clothesline
Underground,
Now free of lice and heads.
These hairs have been treated well
With ammonium chloride, I think.

Afterwards, spread on the floor
Festive and bright under a gun
These will be fit for use,
As felt or lining,
Once dry, casting winter in its dye.

———

Ka-Be

They removed the wrong breast,
A little after you slept.

You wake in the dark,
Eyes adrift like ice floes
In a lake of lids.
Black hair you remember
Dragged
The green stream
Down to the bottom.
Long ago you bent
And touched the shadow
Of autumn that crept
Down the steps
To be with you.

They trace your brow
With a knife,
Bring it down,
Draw a circle around
The other breast,

And hold it there.

Prayer

Tonight the fever burns bright
The symmetry of bones visible
Like loops of tiger-light.

A black swallow collects the dead
Down the smoke-tower of sleep.
The houses are silent,
Angels on pins
Crowd the attic
In confusion.
In the eye of a tear
A crystal cathedral
Travels to its last pier.
Spring depleted breasts,
Helmets of their heads.
The summer carried
The dead by train
To the king.
He wills broken hearts
And shakes the hands
Of orphans.
The earth narrows and splits

Like his forked tongue.
The wind flees on metal wings
The still night and altar,
Onwards to cities of dust.

In my prayer, no one's child,
There is no faith

But your breath,

Faint, uncertain as dawn.

Harbinger

Work the last breath to a loaf of bread.
The axes and spades synchronized, heave
And push. Last night it rained.
From the well of the day
We drew blood.
Each night we come and go
Carrying in our eyes
A little bit of those
Who left behind their jackets
On the hooks.
Into the unknown
They carry their numbers
Which weigh more than the earth.
Shoes, glasses, gods survive
Us. These things
We fear for our children.
Their fingers curl
Like worms around hope.
We step in through a door.
Nothing comes back.

Here we were, in the woods
Far from the earth and echoes.

*

I have arrived alone
Dreaming of this rented room
With a tap,
Close to the tracks.
I can hear the trains brake
And rend
At the unutterable stations
Tending to the journeys' end,
My hands wet with rain
From forbidden lands.

Gospel

His words took your breath away
Blind, he found the home of each message
Unerring, warm. The war was his passage.
Its rites taught him to prophesy the end
Of the day. He knocked on the door
Of the long night prompt as a postman.
We knew him from our dreams.
He wore the twisted cross on his sleeve,
And was dressed in his own surplice.
We won him over with our last loot,
Resisted him
With offerings of the heart;
We read in his eyes
The satisfactions
Of our sacrifices.

Yana

When the shower ends,
You will find me dry
By this hollow pillar of almonds.
Its eyes exhale death.
Through the telescopes
Of screams I will see
The statues of Budapest
Turn green,
My mother in a cowl
Walking the bridge
Under water, where a cross swims
Close to fish.

The air is damp with children's tears.
Once I saw mist rising from stream
And mistook it
For the painware of a dream.

You must pass my chain of gold
To Sasha before he turns naked
Like me.
Between two burnt hearts
Gold stays clear of verdigris.

———

Ledger

The numbers
Tell a story of how they ended
In the shadow of the bird;

Black or white,
Where it falls
The earth is dark.
Tallying,
A million stood
In the rising sun.

A million went

Before it set.

The Time of Our Lives

Dawn betrayed us
Down the hill
Into a pack of helmets;
They taught us little
Or no understanding
In suffering.
The rose reddened
Through our mouths,
We saw the sky nettled.
Nothing was lost to our eyes.
Nothing added
To our lives.
We bled like the evening.
We sang
Like stones.
We turned empty as clocks.

This Close

Let's say we grazed it.
That we could almost push our hands
Through the night
Like the sleeves of a shirt.
That we were to each other
Nearly as real
As in the day's shining mirror.
That we sat hair blowing in the wind,
Knights freed of armour
In sidewalk cafes,
And let the wine burst
In words like grapes.
Saw autumn scorch the trees
In battles lost.
Heard a baby find a foot on earth, cursing.

We were almost here, reeking of our future,
And then we were gone, our hands conjuring
Ashes from the grey air.

―――

Clean Is Good

These petals borne away from bud
Tear pink the dark of laughing wine.
It's for us to see how it might be.
Remember we withstood
The cascade of nights,
And booted days
That lived off us like lice
To pour this out to the masters.

We were many as sands
We measured our lives in grains.
We hoarded ourselves
Over the steppes
Precious as contraband
And entered torn
Through the wind
From teeth to toe
To music.
They sorted us,
Left and right,
Blight and rain,
And we learnt of the fear
Free of salt.
We saw a sign in stealth,
Rein ist fain:
Divining it was death.

Heart

Enemy of the elements and the good earth
I grant you admittance by hammer and abuse
To the stone
In whose heart a clock walks time back
To grey heads popping by the windows.
Their hairy fingers grope
And fumble on clothes
Signalling distress
To far ships suspended
In the ginger sun.
They have forgotten me.
I come from them.

They are blind to the sea,
Their fingers comb the breeze.
That was the place.

When you are done
Winding me down,
Carry back the sea
In your eyes,
Set me free
Where I began.

———

Bridge

The needle threads through your eyes
I've sewn all that you've seen
Into a blindfold
From what the crows gave.
You wave it out of sight
From the other side of the grave.

———

Prize

Arch of his heel spans an empire,
Its rise and fall,
His shadow casts your night.

In the kitchen you arrange
The crumbling cups
Five to a row
And knock them down
With your eyes.

Are those shards
Or icicles? Punctuations in time?

Far from the woods, plucked flags
Misled, like art, a river
Into a battlefield.
A word uttered bereaved
Eternities.
Wreathed in last breaths
Of those who entered
The ice
And stayed under deep,
Iron and helmet,
Preserved
As a war's prize
In permafrost's keep.

Invitation

On a blade of light travels my last.
My friend the executioner stands
At the beginning of his shadow
Reaching through the door ajar,
His head at my feet.

Come, he says,
With me to the courtyard
Where April rages insane
And draws blood from
Everything meant to end.

Tracers

These lines drawn with the long night's eyes
Across the mud and over the mountains pay the price
Searching for a moment that justified the light
Compelling those dear lanes to be visible, bright.

The chimes
Of the church clock
Jangle the air;
And your sister on her head
Against the wall
Seeing the world right,
And you laughing
Bent over.
As if we were forever,

Return,

A letter in a familiar hand,
Slipped under the door
Of a house receding
Along the same lines,
Return to vision
Phantom ache, faded land.

———

Quiet

Conversations in the rain under umbrellas
Urge the world to grow forests, silence.
We are where we are because wounded
Hands folded speech like a prayer
And bright whispers leaved woods.

The trees are still, still the branches wander
In air farthest from roots.
We are where the wind returns shaken

Emptied of heart.

Last Season

By a vulture's light
This art is lit.
October marches
Red
Through day and night.

Hilda, Selma, Ted,
Safe in the arms of Christ,
Collector of bones,
Cleaner of souls;
He combs our hair
With fingers free of guile?

Time rusts human heart
To dust, sprouts tongues of iron
Through erected stone.
Stricken black the trees.
The leaves, flown like birds,
Far from home,
Chat up a storm.

The wind tunnelling
Out of His eyes
Halves us from what's gone.

Arrivals, Departures

Then we came upon a place
Evaporating
Which was neither sea
Nor desert, but an in-between light
Flat as a mat
On which our shadows shimmered
And slept.

Good Friday

The unnecessariness of evil
Is everywhere.
The churning of dead
Into bread;
The hammer, interpreting to bones
The point of the nails;
Sculpted flesh
The statue of a sacrifice,
Hazard at the agony of wood,
The father deserting son.

Suffering blurs the line
Between man and god;
The children strip in silence
To join mothers, termination
Of meetings far too brief.
No word explains, no touch
What it was meant to be.

Still the weeds grope
For light
Towards the moon
Over sleeping stones,
The air coruscated
By an eagle's claw.
You know only fear
Spreading its wings.

The marketplace is the hum
I hear. And through it all
My canary sings.

The years collapse
Like bridges into the river
Of time; I am there, arrested by the hour hands,
Or here, where things are past tending.
Incomprehensible the water,
Receding earth.
The dawn brings bones to light
From the infirmary of the night.
From star to star people scurry
In silent ambulances.
I watch the working of the mouths
The dark bubbling out.

We rise and rise
Towards factories
Where we are made
Through heart beats
Riven to bright beams of light
Issuing endlessly from
His unseeing eyes.

Available Light

(*Ilse Koch was the wife of the Commandant of the Buchenwald concentration camp. She was cruel, and apparently partial to tattooed human body.*)

Ilse, how we come back unerringly to ourselves
For others' sufferings. In Buchenwald, the men
Wore their skin like bangles over their bones,
And some were hanged so their skin wouldn't break.

The sun was blindfolded by wire from their gaze.
Flayed from flesh, in a moment's cannon-flash,
The tattooed dead, you saw, lit the living room
To the desired glow, wrapped around a lamp.

Or filtered, like lace, the cattle cars and smoke,
Falling blows, the children rubbing their eyes
At boots growing tall like turrets in the snow.
And softened, too, the one-way tracks

Like a cross-stitch of steel gleaming
At the heart of things, the twisted sign
Of millions bent on Common Design:
The gas, fatigues, transport, and tanks
The iron nuts and bolts of the human fate.

It takes many, Ilse, and a lot, to keep your room
Just the way you want, put all else to shade.
Often what power does to desire is the same
As what desire does to power; it dims the sight
To available light, so the others flatten formless
To a uniform dark beyond the rim of your lamp,
Their cries faint as emission from the farthest stars.

Price

There he is, a Red Snapper, on a block of wood
Wet with the memory of sea; he is silent as salt, and melting;
All the two feet of him writhing, as if to straighten a thought,
Driven like a hook into his brain, of home, abyssal water.
His eyes roll and close against the world that the sea,
Pouring away like rain from tail and fin as he rose
To the bait, hid like shades, and was astonished
There were rumoured worlds beyond his ken.
Far sounds of praise reach him from the sun
And fall on him like blows to the body of Christ.
His mouth mimes screams
To return home to the cooking depths
That served him right to the last meal
And shaped him tip to lip, packed him perfect
Like a prize. But a fish that caught
Heavens' blinding light must part with the sea
And pay the highest bidder with his life as price.

From *Portraits of the Space We Occupy*

Primary Colour

Peregrine the night
On wings,
Defines motion
And stillness
By intent; assumes
Blindness and rules:
And empire of dispensed justice
Not perhaps free from
Blood, but equal like
Iron is hard or stone
Looks for shape.
Nothing arrests its sway
Born of fierce flight,
Recondite purpose.

Design

First thing in the morning
I think of you.
Your eyes, for instance.

The face though
Is forever forming,
Like patterned panels
Of a blind,
Breaking
At the least breeze.

A thought
Shifting shape
With each ragged breath.

The Sowing Circle

I want to sow some rhododendron seeds. How is it done, and how long does the process take?

It will be several years
Before your rhododendrons reach
Flowering size;
A lot can happen
In between.

Seedlings are like children,

Quite a few of whom
Go hungry in India and Africa,

And show variation
In flower colour, leaf shape
And plant size

One
Out of five kids die in Nigeria
Everyday,
So there is an elemental risk too.
You may invest years in these plants
If you are that sort of person.
If you are kind, a kill is to be had
A beautiful something blooming
Full of faith in its own future
Inspiring all
And this is what makes
Seed sowing so exciting.

From the beginning of January
When winter in many parts
Of the world deepens
Like a pit
Lined with children's hair
To the end of March
Is when to sow the seeds
In a heated greenhouse.

And you will recall
That bottled light whose glow
Haunts you under water
Sometimes when you swim
And thud into a body or two.

Children eager to smile
If only they were
Fed, often may not bloom.

The seed is fine, and needs
To be sown on the smooth surface
Of the compost, which in India
A child will mix for you, peat and perlite
With bare hands, for nearly
Nothing at all, and without looking
Up at you.

Never cover the seed with compost.
Water, and then cover the pots
With a clean plastic bag
To keep in the moisture
As this helps.

Hands cupping little faces
Mothers kissing their children
Hand in hand
Children walking
The air blossoming
With their faces.

The seeds will germinate
In a couple of months
Which isn't much of a period in hope
Once the seedlings are large enough
To handle with care
Prick them out into individual pots.

They should spend the following winter
In a kind place—deny them not water,
In a cool green house—
And be planted out the next spring

And they will throw light

On children as they sing.

Luminous

Or consider the way we hold our hands
Under the wooded night air
So tight as if they might be chopped at wrist
By an axe sprung up from the bleeding roots.

Or the way you search my face as you kiss
Deep enough to know what makes
The leopard's blood leap from spot to spot
And lean back, wounded cub,
Shaking at the thought
This was the rumoured future

We forfeited
At assigned gatherings and waiting halls
Arrivals and departures
Where the spirit balked
And braced without hope.

And we walk the back alleys

Of this accidental town,
Past darkened doorways
And between cold cars
And empty little restaurants

From future and past

Return
By land, sea, and air
By sleight of hand
And turn of phrase
To this wholly present

Moment of grace.

Catch

Head wrapped in a turban of massive fish
Tail down his back and those eyes that have seen
Their last, staring out of his scaly head,
He makes a sales pitch—
To the panicking Churchgate crowd,
Hard put to fix a price on the burden of his wish.

Line of Fire

The blue roads we raced along
Crash into sudden-wrought
Seas, and the desert grows endless
And white as light
Where our feet stopped short
At night.
At our back wind bends
The fine trees we passed under
Root over leaf, extirpation
Of bark from branch.

As we now fall,

Hear the birds cry
And burst into flight

Before we hit the ground.

Alchemy

Fall
With the vulture
In the back, the air under
Its clambered wings
Cold as sleet.
Rise
With the beak
Buried in your brains
Gelid vision.

The world is meat.

Bombay

Highway

We kiss the glass burnished with our breath
Suck syllables from its emblazoned face
And wave, thinking brittle things must break
At entreating touch
Reveal armoured knights, silken
Queens wedged in their laps, teasing nipples,
Loosening purse strings.
Men, women, and crowns brilliant as motives
In escutcheons flashing in the sun when charity
Was a deal our lips might have sealed.
But traffic screeches, where chariots struck fire
And our kisses fall, petals on sheets of burning brass,
We sink deep to our knees and there we rest

And scorching our brow, cavalcade of kings pass.

Professional

Two fingers of the right hand hardened
With filth, stuffed into his mouth, and two of the left
Digging into his bottom, sun-baked Raju
Is working round the clock so both ends are met.

Down at Heel

Someone's father, not mine, took a shine
To the maid, my mother. Gave her the night after
A gift, a pair of shoes mirroring black the sun,
And she said with a smile they were mine.

I squeezed my feet into the polished trap.
The leather vised around my ankles
And bit my toes so hard I ran blind
The long, lone lap around the earth and back.

You will grow into them, he said, and kissed
My mother who was proud I was shod.
I can't walk and inch forward or back, I said,
And ripped off the goddamn hooves
From my flesh. My mother flew
Into a fit, bent down, smelling of him,
And whacked me hard with his gift.

I stared at her through tears
That drowned the sky
Turned and fled past his planted feet
And my heart wore thin at my heels.

That was years ago. I've been on the run
Since, barefoot, crashing through fences
All limbs and hardened heel and sole,
A stampede of one towards the centre of the sun.

Conflagration

Under the flyover
In a hole
Scooped
From the wormwood of night,
Lined by pilfered foam from mangled cars,
Fluff and rags,
Dry as dust
Borrowed babies sleep,
Spent,
Thin stalks and roundheads stacked
In rows like matches in a box
Waiting to flare at the sun's first strike.

Out of Joint

At first they paid me to set the bones right.

In the rock-light of the noon
I piled the newspapers for the knees to rest
And straightened femur, shank and shin
Cracked them right with hand and hammer.

Then the women began bringing in the babies.

Break their limbs
Before they are set, they said,
Liquor on their breath,
Fools parted with their fortune
The quicker
For a broken child.

I brought the brittle bones to light for a while
And my eyes hurt when they cried
And there were strange noises in my head
Like door handles clicking open
Like cisterns flushing.

It got so I left the shanty-town behind

The wood fires
The hot tin roofs
The sulphurous beaches of burnt tyres
The cloud of mosquitoes
And the smoke of flies
The stricken monkey-men see-sawing on their haunches
And the gutter running to the brim in bleak eyes.

Wore my bones thin, walking to this fossil place
A clearing, sand-white and dry, set in the face of the sun.

Where I stood, worms small and black
Crawled in the sun, turned over and died.
It seemed like a burial ground of sorts.
There was a smell, sharp, like iron mated with coal.
It was the worms, of course.
I sat there
Thinking of the prospects of my trade.

———

Sidewalk Art Plaza

These are the hills, remember? Low, blue-black

And trees that laughed white through the night.
What flowers were those? In their fragrance
Our hearts lifted.

There, the little stream.
Cool, clear, in shades of green.
And the congregation
Of fish in thought
Under water.

And these abstractions?
Thaumaturgy of colour
Squares of light sliding
Over one another
Are surely our huts afloat in sunset?

The grass shimmering green, or is it blue,
But tentative, like a flame
And the purple sky in pursuit of the moon.

And there, behind the hedge
The waterfall
Of the Five Rocks.

We've almost forgotten what we left behind.

How familiar the loss.
How distant.

Prospect

While you were looking away
A dog yawned in the sun
And in the distance
A train blindfolded
By a tunnel
Window by window
Regained vision.

I thought of all the things
That could happen
When we are looking away

The universe we miss in a blink.

Ruhnama

Works

Arrived at morning early, by means of this passing thought:
The utter chic of creation, the melon of the sun shot to pieces
In the east by arboreal rifles of long lime-green stems,
Insects whirling through the emerald space of grass
Brash butterflies applauding with wings the arrival of spring,
In the quiet of the dawn, constitute, I submit,
An error in judgement. This sentence of beauty is too harsh.

Then the traffic picked up below the window looking
Over the river clucking against the climbing banks;
Altered my case with alcohol, draped my arse in silk,
Saluted the serried ranks, shook hands with fence sitters
And heard their blood curdle in my rennet-lined hands;
By whip wrought the air with warnings, and set about
Getting my hand in order to the drum of a drunken brass band.
Wanton acts of charity announced my arrival
At the black, glittering Hall Of Annunciation.
Doves rose up towards the fluted loft.
Incense wafted.

Naturally, I offered paradise to all.

―――

Praise

Sonic boom of canned laughter shakes the flakes off the wall.
Last night it was the roof they blew off in merriment.
I deigned the fun, crammed the channels with the pulchritude of
    the place

Naked to the nail, gyrating non-stop to music lifted
From the Moors, and reading false weather reports;
Declared at the diamantine banquet tears unlawful,
Proceeded to bed someone's bride.

The rabble subsides. The lit dark gutters. The face of the night
Dried blue, like the bottom of a bottle drained of ink,
Pressing against their features in thrall to power.

Here, hand us the stamp.

'Look, the king is alming all with his hand, show him a lamp.'

I grind my heels into the faces of the dead, as I pass phalanx
After phalanx of ragged phantoms on their knees
Their upturned faces murmuring a lamentation of thanks.

―――

Benediction

Statues of gold by the score, their armoured breasts prow
The servile air, sunlight cleft by their drawn swords
And crested helmets fall to lesser shades, towers of ivory and glass
Bow beneath their burden,
Affects airs, of amnesty, reason
Beyond reckoning, exhortatory passion,
Point a glabrous hand up north where the orphaned heavens
Trundle along on their splintered axis
Reveal in metal and stone
The multitude of my selves, precious enough to spawn
Their own praetorian guard.

The day is a mirror
And I see myself everywhere.

―――

Penance

This morning again I was drunk with longing for you
And for those days when it was possible to love.

I look out over the terrace, at the minarets of the mosques
From which ascend forlorn cries.
Sounds, like well-worn steps, climbing towards heaven.
(Almost certainly Gods speaks not
English? Persian? Perhaps an argot you forgot?)
What I won was not wholly without value:
Palaces of betrayed kings aflutter
With bat-wings of echoes.
Abandoned ice rinks, the empty railway yard.
The zoo where penguins—the wrong consignment,
It was the spotted deer we wanted—perished in summer,
While in their eyes vision of distant icebergs
Welled up like tears.

I, Curator-king
Of a museum of ruins.

Your hand was cool to the touch, and I was the crystal
Your breath would mist over and dissolve.
Into an eternal gaze of longing.
We might have been two against the world.
You denied me your all. I denied myself.

I left the Durbar in a state, and groped my way to the washroom.
There they found me gagged by the shoe of a commode.
I was sick. That night, in sleep, I swore myself into a kind of penance

Abjured dreams.

Global Warning

Driven by drought
The poor do their rounds
Past the archway of precious stones.
Exiled from hallowed grounds
They carry on their shaven heads wattled roofs.
Their kettles and drums make empty sounds
As they struggle past festal lights, feral guards.

The naked girl's face over her father's shoulder
Follows me like a stare.

I pour myself behind my glares
Retreat, shaken, to my lair.

———

Red Tape

And what's to be made of the poet,
His many fine words and broken utterances
Resonating in trapped ventricles of air,
Horses of terracotta and huts of mud, surviving in tatters
Colonnades of polished stone pouring themselves into the sands?

The day retracts vision into reddening lids, these ruins wreathed
In shadows aggregate the last bastion of leaden sight, coppery fields
Of livid, defeated light.
Strapped to his overnight bag, and stuck beneath
His matted hair, he looks prophetic or merely pretentious?

The stars tapped into ink-blue page of night
Like creation's code
Are all that he wants to decipher. What if he would maim himself
For a little fame? And contrived to kill for scattered applause?
Off with his face then, or empty a bag of black scorpions over his head
And let their concerted sting tell his tale? Or neglect him merely?
Which will kill him more?
I set aside the file, listened to shadows shrift in the sand.

Bollywood

Remember in detail, the arrival of the powdered two-page script
Ushered in by a footman fey with attitude, engraved in gold,
Set in a silver case, enumerating fourteen synchronized dances
Down an alpine slope, setting off an avalanche of costumed starlets;
Siblings separated at birth, the missing treasure-trove
The tattered map, and the captive king loud in his decrepitude.

The project flourished among its well-wishers who drank copiously
With a view, I think, to escape the tiger-terrors of lucidity.
I assured all help, in a swoon greeted the leading ladies, and struck
    a deal
With the pleonastic producer whose latex suit reeked
Of saurian piss. Or was it perfume?

The Empire would be a neoteric studio. The rivers of lasers,
The vegetation plump with rain, the four seasons and the snow at
    X-mas
A matter of technique, the casual theology of make believe.

In the land where I was king, salvation by eye for those
Who weren't fastidious was now free, and went begging

On the chimera-streets agog with their own desert delusions.

External Affairs

The weather grated, rough rag. A rock outcrop furrowed
From out of the sand, a gash in the desert's flank.

Beyond it, the low limestone hills shimmered close to the earth's rim.
An occasional flash from a mirror or gun harbingered the break
In the enemy's stupor a change of mind. In between crouched
A patch of crated land shaped like a tiger about to spring, a heritage
Lowered intact from the ancient loft of Mars.

Habit or need, we fought over it. The air embattled
With war cries bared a perspective, but yielded no judgement
The young and the old arrived in fatigues and fell to their end;
Our patriots were their betrayers, but crusade or pillage
What they sought blurred the distinction.

On holy days we ceased from the fatal exertions; the chiefs feasted
Even, together, drank to the kings, judged laughter-shows
Staged by vaudevillian soldiers, counted the change the dead left
    behind; shook hands, slept.
The land lay smouldering in the moonlight, beyond dispute and
    claim.

―――

Thrift: A Letter to the Mayor

Off the town centre, roses raddling the burden
Of the cross by a window amaze
With their exhalations
The already unnerved public.

Please investigate their provenance, the cause of their conduct
(A lewd levity of manner?), possible profligacy
On the part of the proprietor, her resources, the quantity of water
Rare even in remembrance, gone into the grooming of the spectacle

As also the mystery of the torn face

Exfoliating among the carnations crowned with thorns.

———

Drop Out

A storm howling and straining at an invisible leash.
Suspension of the desert in mid-air. Rain plonking it back to earth.
All of it took time. And so the schoolchildren were late to arrive
For the Friday oath of allegiance.

I eased out on to the balcony
And was gratified; blessed the Ruhnama scholars.
The prefect was bright, and made bold to present me with a poem,
A rhyme in praise of my reign. I let him sing

And recalled with surprise my inability to read or write.

———

Curriculum Vitae

I pronounced my needs as if they were prophecies.
The protocol of power just, as I was the chosen one.
Forayed into the chiaroscuro-terrain of fair play to my delight
Affected reserve in craven company for grander praise.
Baffled by my random impulse to defile women,
I focused on steady pillage. It was much less the trouble.

Fed stray dogs and fought back,
Mouth working, bouts of depression as dawn bared its fangs.
My doubts were a religion, and I was my own squirming god;
At any rate, succeeded in keeping up appearances
And reflected idly on the back seat of my Maybach:

Was I born like this, a mask, or did it fall from the skies
And visor around my face, perfectly in place?

A Shortage of Words

Once, when I was eleven and some
I was caught stealing a Max Brand
From a rental library. The old man
Who kept the place took me out
Into the sun
And slapped me so hard
Mirrors skittered in my head
And I could see myself endlessly
Everywhere.

Don't tell anyone, I told him, walking
Backwards, staring at him all the time,
Don't tell anyone.

A couple of years later in high school
I ran a raffle with money out of my pocket.
You see, I liked to surprise my friends with gifts.
After the first draw, the headmaster called me
Into a high room cold, the only source of heat
Was my palm, burning red
Every time his rubber-wrapped cane
Descended to set fire to my flesh.
Go tell your friends, he said.

Around this time, my father, a Communist
Plotting at revolution, became fed up
With the breakfast I never ate,
And took a stick and beat my bare back
About like a bush, till birds of pain flew up in the air

And the stick in his hand broke.
He was beat.
I called out to his retreating back blank like a door,
I'll tell everyone,
I'll tell all your friends.

When I was twenty, and a drunk,
The police caught me for travelling
Without a ticket which I had.
Later they changed
Their grievance to prevention of discharge of duties
And beat the shit out of me because I was drunk
And angry as my girl
Was putting the answering machine on me.
Tell her, I said to them, tell her.

Well, there have been other instances
Of violence taking over speech.
But now that I am forty, I no longer care
Who has the right of tell.

I think now
Each blow to the body is a word
Deleted from the dictionary.
That's why
We don't have more words than we deserve.

Catafalque

'I go as the first, at the head of many (who still have to die); I go in the midst of many (who are now dying). What will be the work of Yama (the ruler of the departed) which today he has to do unto me?– Nachiketa to his father, in Katha-Upanishad, who in a fit of anger gifted him to Yama, the Ruler of the Dead.

Post Natal

A room secreting smells
Laundered linen
Breathing out camphor.
Old Spice, old books, soap ghosting
Air with scent of rose.
Blue ink gleaming thick in vat of glass,
On the roll-top desk, the fat green pen on its side, run dry and smoking
Where it stopped. Lunar blips gilding the corner basin of water.
The floor waxed black verging on the brink
Of light, a dark pond mirroring the advance of the night.
Wet whiff of a body wasting.

My father on the cot in white, straight as a corpse in a coffin.
The hours crawl about him in ambush
Detonating memory cells at each intractable breath
Burning synapses down like a bridge
Weighting his tongue down
With speech slush.

Between flashes he wakes up blind, shakes a hand at the carnage
Laying him bare to the crib. Remembers neither the revolt
Of the beginnings, nor the submission at arrival. Between birth
And death, there's nothing. Not even sorrow.
My father is a big baby, born today, gone tomorrow.

Eclipse

His fingers, like tendrils
Coil the air about without a care.

His feet he carries after him
Heavy, haphazard
Like an afterthought.

His speech dies at birth.
If hyoid is a bone,
He picked it clean a while ago.

He sits in a heap, wan, a smiling slave
To gravity
Pulling him down to the grave.

His eyes arrive at sight
Slow, hesitant, strangely bright
See the world in their leftover light.

———

Favour

Caught in the cross hairs of a farewell sun
At the far end of a long passageway
He sits or stands, moves or pauses
Comes or goes, as you please.
Clad or otherwise, he's naked
To the eye.
He is not here or yet the far there
Where shadows sleep.

If you were a good son
You'd hold to his head
A steady gun.

Threshold

The roses are on their own.
The grass spreads
Like water from an upturned urn.
Between mornings smudged blue like bruises
And evenings bubbling like blood
Along the broken arteries of the sky
The road narrowing through hedgerows,
Hens, fallow fields, darkening stream
Slows towards home to halt
At my father's feet, far from town.
He clasps his hand over his head,
The softening crown.
And I see
His hands are no longer hard or brown.

Rout

At first, you did not let on
Bent over the rampart of your desk, an old king surveying
What's left, the sunlight flagging white the paper
On which you were surrendering, face close
To the fabled pen, the last of the language you lived by
Writer redivivus, inhaling ink, memory's blue blood.

I look over your shoulder at the random craft
Practicing on you its witchery
And see with eyes that praised the kingdom
You set up once with your phrases
Mutant shapes, in singles and droves, freak alphabet
Of forgetfulness, while your hands shake in time's fetters.

Permanent Revolution

April now in the Kremlin, machines part
Late snow on either side, soft white hair falling
Away to reveal the black scalp of the road.

The wall of the Square
And all that's red when it was bright
Congeals like clotted blood into the night;
Everything except the snow.

Here in April, the eviscerated earth
Awaiting your arrival rolls down
A carpet of cracks. You are the filling in the blanks.
In the tonsuring solar fire of the South,
Leaves curl like smoke.
Flame of the forest is a Franciscan Friar.
Only the bougainvillea rouses the rabble-air
With its speech of blood.

If this is your last summer, do you give a damn?
Speak. Do you, sir, remember
All that you said in praise of the USSR?
Of the Kremlin, Lenin, Red Star?
The thirty books you wrote, now footnotes
To a history that was false? How see now
Your passion for that which was not?
The faith no God could shake?

Such illusions that make us brave
We carry to the grave.
Go down, and still find rest
In the shade of the red flag
Follow the shining star
To worlds revolving beyond summer and snow
Assured, in Moscow, embalmed Lenin sleeps
Dead as you, and dressed to kill again the Czar.

Pogrom

Go in rage. Or in umbrage. Go with the wind, or fire.
Become one with the earth. You and I are dust.
It's nothing. In dust we trust. The thread of blood
That ties us up in knots is nothing. If it's not you
It'll be someone else who raised this roof
And later brought it down.

Now the children seem something.
Ah, they grow faster than you can dry their hair,
See soon the flakes of white in their stubble,
Like snow glimmering in green woods.
Eventually they too will be shaven dust.

Nothing is dust scattered in the cosmic storm.
We conduct ourselves to that one norm.

Chutney and Gruel

Out of the album slides a snap
Black-and-white, time-spotted, with the porch
Of the old house, now dug up to the last stone,
At the back.

And two kids held to sullen truce
And a mother making love to the camera
As if she was always going to be the star
No matter if the movie was never made
And you in the middle, in a loose shirt,
Tennis-collared, top button undone
Mouth set, both eyes shut.

It was not the flashing bulb
Nor the sudden word bursting
In the mind like hot light
That blinded your eyes
To a crease.
It was the third meal always cruel
In coming
When we stepped out of frame
Ceased to be a picture,
Asked for milk, cheese;
Chutney and gruel.

I Spy

The letter I wrote to you when I was
Eleven about my mother,
Felicitator of fatalities, her manic acts
Of high-handedness, profligacy, bouts
Of mocking laughter
And how you must save me,
Perhaps come down from Madras
Where I thought you were dispatched
As a spy for the Soviet Union
Or were you just reporting for TASS
(But that'd be just too ersatz)?
Well, that was the mail I sent you,
Spy to spy, you my mentor
Which you returned, too,
Post-haste to my tormentor
Who turned again to her
Implements with a razor-smile.

If only you had torn that letter and blown
It to the wind, I might have grown up less alone.

I

I who hid my face in the wear you left
In the basket for wash, Cuticura
Mixed with sweat, Old Spice, Brylcreem
On the side, so your casket of odours
Would bear me through the night's dark tides.

I who went around the ancient house papering
Over cracks through which lizards of light
Crept, and closing windows so I was free
For a while longer from the gaze of those
Who slept, except you who asked what it was
With me about light, and I said, I was afraid
Of others awaking too early in my world.

Now, as I stretch myself to dim your lamp
And close the window on the other side,
If you asked me
What it was about the light
As when I was in the first grade
The answer still is, I am afraid.

———

Oedipus Vexed

From long ago, a day, like a door in halter
Swings out from monsoon stable.
I open a blinkered eye
And still hearing
Echoes from a whole life lived
A minute ago
In an evening the colour of brass
Of wild hooves thudding over a wet black track

See my father naked, his penis big and slack
Shuffling his way to the washroom
Across the courtyard in the early dark.

I gather sleep around me like a blanket
Wishing out the day in the wink of an eye
Returns safe to fields where horses fly.

Post Crypt

The letter you wrote when you were thirteen
Expressing concern for your father's health
His foundering fortune
One hand on orphaned heart, the other pushing
The early pen, that he may yet find,
In his paternal reserve, enough to draw for ink
And paper, a fresh lease,
So you may continue your studies, please,
Has reached me this morning, seventy years later
While shifting your books and such closed chapters
Including the one on the boy who dropped out of school.

I'd like to tell you: I'm in a position now
To honour your request that cast a shadow
On your father's face and raised his brow.

―――

Statue

Whose statue is it in the dry fountain
Disfigured by truant stone or hand of time
Brought to this pass
The curlicues
Of his name altered by flung mud
From where he too must come
But the City's Father
Quiescent to the weather, birds,
Children's laughter,
Before he died, and was born again
Brow beaten, encased in stone.

I return home to see your face
At the darkening window
Staring at your son with eyes
Opening in another world
Passing into disuse:
A monument true to its ruin
With a smile too vague for an epitaph.

Homage to a Hen

Once upon a time, at first light, you set out to the post office
To mail a report which you did with a satisfaction
That conjured up from a sidewalk café, fried eggs, sunny side up
Fluffy as a cloud on a day in spring. I can still feel the buds
That bloomed on my tongue, and I never
Had a breakfast like that since, which made me sing.
If that day was an empire, I was king.

Today I was up at dawn
To tell you that a hen that laid such timeless eggs
Deserved a hug, but was brought short
At your door
Behind which you lay wholly beyond recall.

Dog

The last time I saw you happy
You had lost your way on a visit
To the city, and as the morning
Mourned into noon, you returned home
Tired as a dog back from the woods,

With a stranger at heel, who said,
No, not to mention, it was part of the game
He too had a father like mine,
But put a collar on him, he said, a name
And an address, so people know
Where he comes from, where to go.

That's all I needed, my father said,
Rolling over, tongue out, playing dead.

Face to Face

I worry about your mind vacant like your shelves
Once lined with books, files, awards, now gathering dust,
Under whose ceaseless pouring weight we bend and merge
Formless underground, emptied of ourselves.

Full Circle

Stillwater, grey blue. The low hills still,
Grey, blue, too. The sky liquescent,
Pale green, languid, lavender streaked.
Nothing was ever like this.
A pendant floating
Out of the broken sun,
Towards far trees
Is birds
Before breaking into a coma
In flight.

Perhaps there is no full-stop,
We are a trick of the eye
Ever arriving
Though we may think we are cast in stone.
In time, this winged jewel we will wear
Around the neck when we become air.

Portraits of the Space We Occupy

Once on the frieze, framed pictures
Of Gandhi nearly threadbare conspiring
With Nehru roseate. At an arm's distance
Lenin incarnadine, leaning out from a labour pulpit.
Stalin chewing the steel in his cigar. Native Communist leaders:
    Krishna Pillai,
His features carved in stone,
A.K. Gopalan in need of testosterone.
And next to him you, in a blue jacket with red trimmings smiling
    at the shy Russian girl
Of five in your arms.

Her name was Indira,
After Mrs Gandhi when she was P.M.
Since you turned your own pale ghost
We've carried them all up to the attic
Leaving behind on the wall empty squares of light.

Beyond the garden where dogs bark
I can hear a lone child cry.
Shall I tell her, set no store by what you see,
We are just portraits of the space we occupy?

Boy

The great man you wanted me to become,
The world's best surgeon or some such,
A success story that suffered no disgrace,
Brought his father pride,
At this late hour come back making light
Of the promises not made good.

Here I am finally,
Short, bearded, bald; a veined hand
Pinned under a tattooed cross
Placating in vain the heart's swell
At your tide turning in, the other
Holding yours, wishing you well.

———

Sound Proof

Each day is a padded door shut
In my face, the other side of which is you.
How shall I make you hear the music
Of the grass growing silent as dew?

———

Gastronomy

We ripen through the rain, carrion for the crow
The night wedged between wings, beak, claw.
What it spits out in red surfeit is what you saw
With your eyes, felt in your heart, the white of snow,
Leaves lit like candles long after the sun had set.

Bow down to the bird, its hunger is all God.
The ache at parting, clod from clod,
Is all Man, the father or son bereft.

Vision

Three lost kings, crowned by an upturned umbrella, arrive
Late, as the day drowns in rain, to offer respects to the man
They might have taxed or served when he was not in so much pain.
Flowers in hand, they stand around you
In form and shadow. You stare at them for long, one at a time,
      your face tense:
Old Age singling out
Friend from foe in dying fire-light.
At last, you turn your head,
Return blind to the burnt-out mind.

Who Shifts the Stars So June Is Here Again?

Who shifts the stars so June is here again?
Moist light, virginal breath and petal-eyes wide
In wonder, she is tugging at the damp door.

The bridge you walked on, closes under water
And the fish now swim over the road. The leaves
Lush with rain are lovely beyond reason.

Burn at hearth like fire
Redden the embers with your dying breath.
Last the beauty of this sodden season.

Guest

And the days pass into weeks, and months into years
And up the winding stairs approach footfalls
Growing loud like heart beats in our ears.

Translation

Shadows drift under the street lamps,
Merge and pass. If it were thus, pared of flesh
And bone, what matters it who heads the batch,
Who at the centre, marching towards Yama?
You showed me the earth. Now each difficult breath
You draw weighs me down with what you gave.
I am in debt to all I see and hear, paddy glittering
Green in the field of day, the stream plucking its way
Through stars, the moon caught in flight in a throng
Of thorns. Your gifts are at work even after death.

Time effects its slow translation of the original
Into elements, the living text's various versions.
I must bow down to the ground I tread,
Recall with grace what's lost as you pass
Into the earth and air, holy as the Host in bread.

From *Canaries on the Moon*

Extraterrestrial

It was different
Where I came from.

Dumb suffering wasn't the dark well
From which you drew silence.

There would be no gates

In an ideal world
There would be no Nike.

Nobody would be
At the mercy of others' fates.

Everything would be something.
And nothing led to anything.
Point bore no stretching
There'd be no geometry.

I look out of the window,
Thinking, it's time for rocketry,
Time to go. I returned
To the beat up mother craft

Looking forward to flying again

Canaries on the moon
And other fine arts of aliens grown daft.

A Drop

Bubbled out of the sun

Drew a bead
On earth,

Startling the stars

With its intent.

Birds
Tried to catch
It around their necks

A pendant for prey
To gaze at themselves
Through the mists
Of their last breath.

Monsters and men
Swooped after it
To wear it in their eyes;
A glimpse of heaven
From their living hell.

But it glittered

Past their worlds.
The drop entered
The orbit of the earth
With a smile so cool
It snowed in the tropics.

The drop paused
For a second
And then fell
Into his praying hands,
Sparkling.

He weighed it, gingerly,
Like a flame,
Tossed it aside,
Wondering at its name,
Renewed waiting.

The drop
Poured back from here
Into the centre of the sun
The clouded eye of time
Hurting with its one unshed tear.

A Necessary War

Guns upon a time

There was a king
So strong
The sea pulled back its ears
Surrendered her suckling waves.
She licked his feet
When he strolled
On the beach.

The king was so brave
Lions mangled their roars
Into silence deep inside
The death-well of their throats.

The king loved peace.
Guns and swords and horses
Developed rust and moss and fleas.

But a time came,
When peace was threatened.
To defend it,
The king made sacrifices.
He began with cattle
And ended with men.

It was either that or war.

But the soldiers
With their eyeballs smoking
In their palms
And bits of steel grinning
Between their teeth
And their brains steaming
With what they had left
Behind at home

And hair like terror spiked
And skin shiny with death's oil
Couldn't understand
What cleaved them from the grass.

But it didn't matter.

The king went for his stroll.
Bereaved evenings
Followed him like a cloak.
The sea behaved, fastened to breeze.

It was so very quiet, it felt like peace.

Season Flipping

I bequeathed the orange
To my healthy but senile father.

The scissors I handed over to my sister.
Someday she will find a use for it.

Rope and the bucket to my wife.

My briefcase to my son
With one little finger in it.

There was some money, small change,
I willed that to charity.

Having given away all
I sat back in the ambulance
Alarming the evening air,
Feeling rich.

As I sped,
Keen to the weather,

Summer was turning
To autumn through the leaves,

The sky a pale green.

Parli

Exile and the Kingdom

Through with the washing,
She leans back in the air,
Holding aloft a white sari,
Over her head like a flag,
The breeze from the river
Unfurling her kingdom's
One red, solitary star.

I gaze at it from afar.

Daze

Emerging from sleep,
A shower of powder
In the tall, cold drink
Blazing pink.
Glucose icing
Melon's blood,
Hot weather-shrink.

Emerging from wake,
A serpent circling
The neck of the hill
Roars out a lion of cloud
Into noon's tawny dust:
Heat shaking out its beast.

Emerging from the roar, a song
From the cinema sowing
Memories like seeds
In paddy fields.

Emerging from the song, a woman
Laughing like a lamp
From a window in the dark.

Emerging from the dark
Behind a rock
A pyre:
The living disappearing
In a glare.

Emerging from the glare
A clear cold river in your face
Sudden like a slap:
The moon plopping into water.

All my life emerging
From the slap,
Stung,

Counting stars.

———

Asthma

I trace my anxiety
To what I lacked
When I was born
In June
In a room sodden
Like a wet blanket:
The airless space

I carry wound,
A fold a day
Everyday
Over my face like shroud,

Gasping for breath.

Replenishment

A river white as a rabbit
Bolts from my feet swollen
Dark with the places I have been.

She bounds up the low hill
Scurrying back under the railway tracks
And leaps at me endlessly over a rock.

I dive under and come up
In water, my nails shining
White with the light of places I will go.

Blow by Blow Account of a Boy Missing

When my toes curled, the hills awoke.

When I stretched, the river surged.
When I set out, the earth galloped
I widened my eyes, the sky was a movie.

When I drew water,
Gravity dreamt
A well on wings.

I plucked mangoes,
Seasons swelled in my fist

I stole candies,
A volcano of sugar
Erupted
In my mouth.

I mated, mirrors went blind.
I rested, the breeze blew in the masseurs.

I slept again, a child went missing.

———

Soldier

Returning by train
Through a tunnel of trees
The river flashes by my side
A sword endlessly drawn
From an endless sheath of green.

———

A Quick Brown Fox

There's a quick brown fox about.
It jumps over lazy dogs when folks type.

This morning I saw him, trotting
Down the hill, across the fallow paddy field.

He came in through the front door
Went to the study across the hall

Nosing open my father's blue Olivetti,
Looking up and down the rolled in paper,

Which said, the quick brown fox jumped
Over the lazy dog. I told my father

About the fox and his nose. He said,
Foxes like to read about what they do.

For a while back there, I believed that too.

———

Bless and Curse

Now that you say, eyes drawn
Like a kite to the sky, you don't love
Me, I'll have this mire married
To the bog this monsoon.

Now that you say we are different people,
I'll have every mountain turn a stone
Every tree a sling,
Catapult the earth flat, make it all the same.

Now that you are going away
I'll have all doors spy on their shadows
Deny the sun the keyhole of my heart
Wear the endless night
Like glares over sight.

Now that you have taken away
What you gave,
I'll resist to the end
With what's left behind
The instant ageing
Of a boy's blood
The loss of wonder

A turn of mind.

Coffee

They sat at Grey's drinking coffee,

They looked everywhere
Except at each other, sipping,
And stirring the void between them

With the spoon, frequently adding sugar
As if to sweeten what had gone sour.

Passover

There was a kitchen cooking.

The sun rose from the oven and lit
Butter, bread red, and cherry like blood,
Stacked in crystal bowls and plates.

Children sat around wearing pitiless smiles
And harbouring secrets long as miles.

Then my sister, denied of lipstick
The night before, pulled
The table-spread out:

A wave of white,
The dishes riding its crest,
Before it crashed.

On the floor each crumb of the feast shone:
Cherries with shards in their heart
Butter and bread spiked with glass.

Each King in His Place

Last time I dropped in at Paradise Bar
Nothing had changed, not a lint,
Nor the fake samovar.
The King was sipping
Vodka with crushed ice,
Lemon and mint.
His girls brought up on strawberries
And cream
Were skating on ice
Slow as if in a dream.
Business as usual
For the team.
Only, the man
In the cage
Playing the violin
Wearing a bow
Behind the curtain of lace,
Wore another face.

I put it down to variations on a theme.

Statistics

A man couldn't remember his name.

He had lost it letter by letter
To the language of many wars.

The man went around looking
For his name,
But everything looked the same.

He thought it was a memory
But his mind was a misty mirror
Shifting in a maze.
He thought it was a flower
But he couldn't recall its bloom.
He thought it was a bird
But he couldn't place its call.
He thought it was an animal
But it was hard to figure out its habit.
He thought it was a season
But he couldn't see its drift.
He did think it was a man
But he couldn't tell one from another.

Could it be a stone?
What was its shape?

A river?
But water no longer spoke.
Fire?

Why was it no different
From his silence?

He tried re-christening himself.
But what was in a name?

He gave up. Returned to war.
Became a boot.

Swelled the ranks.

A Nightmare

A nightmare tore around,
Looking for a medium.
Found one at last
In a rabbit
In a clearing
Flat as a stadium.

So then the rabbit
Ran, heart and blood and brain racing
Against each other, till her whole body poured
Into a blur.
The ripple of her run played
Like lightning against the black fur,

Picking its way through
Pyramids of teeth

With tails,
And a hundred legs
That wild dogs grow as they hound
A rabbit on the run.

The dogs had been dreaming
There was a rabbit ripening like a plum
In the sun
Just for them.

She ran and skipped and swerved and rolled
And broke her run with a scream.
Which is how the nightmare ended.

The dogs tore her speed to shreds
The throb in her thighs, the light in her eyes
The full heart and brain

The space she shaped like clay
The dogs put to another use.

Then they lay down heavily

Gazing at the light.

Dire

Bat

Dread-alert in the middle of the night
Pinned to my bed,

I listen to the dark growing wings:
Flying from out of time, a baby bat
Thudding against the walls,
Keening for its mother

A glowing sound somewhere

In the nest of blind hours.

Parody

In the bathtub a whale-shark, mean
Flat headed. A hammer if you knew
How to wield it. On the washbasin,
An ill-looking vulture. Snakes coupling
On the balcony. The usual numbers
Of the glasses drunks wear.
I come back to my whiskey, relieved,

It's not over yet. Not by a long shot.

Futile

The lion met him,
In a delirium of compassion
Shook its mane scattering
Through the prism of day petals
From the clotted rose of a kill
And said, it's you,
Or the one you love.
Choose.

Eat me, he said, cowering.

The noon yawned,

The lion slept.

Eat me, he said, again
Offering, despite himself,
The full menu of one dish

When the lion awoke.

No, the lion said,
I've changed
My mind.

It's the other meal I want.

He sat next to the lion, feeling old,
And futile as a dinner going cold.

Pause

Mad dog streaking
Through traffic
Looks back
Trembling
At the interminable
Accident
At his heels.

Cambridge, Autumn

The agony
Of being
Blind

In a beautiful place.

Kalki Brimming

The kneecap was the drum.
Thighbone stick.
Vultures nesting in the crook of the elbow.
Fire and filth piling up in the heap of the eye.
A plum-dark sea roiling in the veins.
Marbles stacked in the hollow of the bones.
Serpents coiling in the grotto of the groin.
Thrust through the skull a lit torch.

Sour wine in cupped hands.
A man in full,
Looking for more.

———

Stone

Footprints on stone
Stone paves the way.
Starlight on stone
Stone lifts its eye.
Caveman's axe tests stone
Stone's teeth smile fire.
Dogs piss on stone
Stone gives up ghost.
A worm turns stone
Stone laughs down the slope.
Rain licks stone
Stone turns throne to moon.
Wind hammers stone
Stone sheds its masks.
Man considers his brother.
Stone cries out to God.
A leopard dreams.
Stone speeds to fat-land.
Supine, a woman gathers her bruises,
Stone's a quiver of screams.
A thief steals behind stone
Stone hides him like a treasure.
Shadows fall from the sun
Stone frees its captives.

But why is stone so hard?

Because of its song.

Why is stone so quiet?

Because its voice is a shape.

When will stone rest?

When Earth returns to star.

———

News in Brief

Search for spanner goes like a bomb.
Hunter of rocks hardens heart.
The door is on its own.
Lonely heart loses all.
President reveals his past.
People lose their vision.
Tiger rests his teeth in water.
Season spreads trees.
Suicide admits to last thoughts.
Not even grass grows.
Bubbles rise to rainbow.
Road races through shut eyes.
Reluctant arrow misses meat.
Game marked before hunger growls.
Through hoops cats go black.
The day goes up in screams.
Under steel and mud

Boy hugs himself, found.

———

Reading Glasses

Wearing the well-framed word
Over his eyes
He saw the Universe
Either smaller or bigger
Than it was,
But never once

For what it is.

Aasa Khosa

Met him on Marine Drive, walking
In sleeping-clothes, on his way

From Srinagar,
Four days by train,
Where he had a house.

It exploded.

There was a garden too,
That hissed down like a match in water.
Just flared and was gone in the war.

Not to mention
Two sons and a wife
Who went missing
In the grocery shop.

Enough things to make a man
Not believe
In god and country; make him walk
In sleeping-clothes all his life.

Khosa said, looking at the sea,
He had acquired
A recent problem
With his eyes, they took a long time
Focusing.
Like just now, he took a long time
Focusing on the sea.

When he finally got a fix on it,
He said, remembering everything
Behind his eyes, it's hard to believe
Your life's your own. If someone told you
The story of your life when you were
A child, you wouldn't have believed it.

Perhaps, we are all leading
Other people's lives, he said.

Yes, that's it, everything's somewhere else
And I'm so far away.

Waiting

There are a few things I need to tell you.
But to do that, I must grow first the heart
Of a lion and his iron lungs.
The tongue must learn to spout flame,
Throw it high over the vast waters of silence,
Set your laughing flesh on fire
On the other shore.

That's just for starters.

The words then. The words must
Speak sabre, a language tigers growl
When they have their prey nailed
In hunger's cross-hair.

What I have to tell you is a story;
A story of beasts
Trapped in the zoo of my body, waiting
For me to speak the language of their rhapsody.

———

Rumour

I want the rain to hold me for so long
I can think clearly in the cold
That things considered necessary
For so long

Don't matter.
That when I grow
And my teeth chatter

I'll still pace the floor
Of a house fond of me
And listen to the clarity

Of rain taking root in the air
Growing forests without fuss.
A heavy, steady rain washing me clean

So compassion flows
Though the light
Of my terminus glows.
A conviction
It cannot have been any other way
Than this need to watch the rain

Shaking foliage
Through the arid years
Of age.

A rain, darkening tiles
Loosening the earth;
Stone tubs in the garden
Brimming, bubbles to buds.

Everywhere water banishing
The world beyond to a rumour.

From *Posthumous Poems*

Toast

Chance queen of tonight, Ms Christopher
Drop your glass and hold my hand.
All that I write is to get one word right.
It kills. But death doesn't matter.
It's metaphor.

Night Vision

In my sleep the trees whirled
And leaf by leaf light emptied.
When I awoke everything I liked
Looked alike.

The Family Court

At the Family Court
The lift would not work.
So they walked up
Four flights
Of stairs and passed
On the fourth landing
Two toilets, one marked,
For Judges Only, and one,
For Others. They used
The first though.
But no one charged
Them with contempt of court.
Later, they sat in the hall
With some twenty others,
People come together
To be separated.
The four fans in the hall
Big as windmills
Breezed past
Their several lives.
Late in the noon
An attendant
Called out their names
And led them into a hall
Where the judge
They met in the toilet said
They were no longer
Man and wife.

Goal Keeper

Hurtling through the shadows in the grass
Teasing abuse from spikes, rounded hide,
Dead beast tanned, despairs home
Past my outstretched hands towards
Prophecies of trestle and cordage. Goal.

Once again the universe cartwheels
And other sidereal prospects, coaches,
Broken ties, hotel rooms spin out of focus.
From the ringed stands, a trillion cheers raise
A tower to the sun. Under the crossbeam, I sink

On knees of water, eyes composed to darkness
Through a wreath of sudden pain. Monarch
Of empty air, I leave impress upon space
With a sigh, of a far truth breathing close
And borne away in the same breath:

Implosion of all time in a moment's dare
And miss; a whiff of eternal loss.
Back the ball goes, kissing boots in gratitude
To its shifting flight from loyalty to treason,
as the soldiery dip, rise and dance,

Work their antagonism towards wine.
What they kick about lies close to my heart
But never fellowship of conscript dust.
I relapse into vigil-crystal, gaze at my goal,
Ice-embalzoned solitude its future and resolve.

Return

Today I shaved, the air my mirror.
Bathed in the river, the falls my shower
Listened to music, the wild grass my violin.
Blessed trees for fruit pure as fire.
Pulled the sky over my face, spoke to the stars
And slept on sand, the breeze my song.
The moon was easy, moving through the branches
Of my bones.
Tomorrow at first light, I'll cut my wrist

Watch a perfect sun, set.

Anchored by a Hare's Breath

Enter dawn through a crack in her eye,
But she's lost to him in a dream
Of colours flowing
Like a levitating stream.
She'd be airborne, drift past him,
Be gone, but for her toe
Which from under the fraying horizon
Of the bunny blanket
Coils the engrossed air
Around a chipped nail
Like a taut wire.

Thief

Crabwise this grief grows
Back to a passage owned by the wind.
Paddy dried on the floor
The air smelt of Oveltine.
In the corridor, clothes on the line
Few about like trapped birds
With large wings.
They changed colour as the day wore on.

Thieves hid in corners, hatching
Laughter and secrets.
They restored to externed adults
Chains of glass beads and gold,
Inventing crime

Whose betrayal occurred when veins
Clogged, and blood thickened.

But we walked that passage once,
Knew crimes to be close to dreams.
So I close your eyes with the colours
We saw, and watch you steal into the fire
With the glass beads and the gold.

Dedication

Round, gnarled, tough and tall
The well-branched pursuit
Swims above all; mediates silence,
At ease in the arranging of space.
Grows deeds in gleaming foliage
Disowns virtue at vertigo hour.
Ripeness falls. When the fifth wind blows
Lays down arboreal arms,
Breaks back to bole.
Abstinence from the self,
Order in wood.

War and Peace

Under the fog-lights and domes of the city
A million men at war hurry home,
And make peace, tossing a bomb
In the living room.

In Good Company

Sometimes I imagine under the floor,
There must be a whole graveyard
Buried along with its severe norms of silence,
Observed at the passing away of a language
That once faintly breathed in the images
Of the flesh; made speech seem possible
When the full moon rose through the trees
Like a frisbee without stop.
The dead are beyond reaching out, words;
They are perfect; trying doesn't become them.

So tonight, the two of us will sit
Across this yawning table,
Each sworn to a just silence,
Dead in bed and out of it,
And drink a little ahead of time
To those who lie right
Under our feet and stare at our soles.

Contentment

There was pity for the self.
This was easy,
And some mistook it for remorse.
Through all a bitter wind blew
Turning brother against brother;

Bramble, branch and rush burned.
Their ashes scattered like flies,
Whirled back together in the wind.

Doors kept closing, likewise windows.
The fishermen were not fertile.
The sea sank. Those who worked in fine flax,
Those who wove networks, were confounded.
Knives didn't cut.

As for birds, they flew where the wind blew.
Hearing them was like the wall wailing
In Jerusalem. The air was blind
With searching wings, floating mirrors.
Breathing was an exercise in blue.

Angels aching to shake a leg
Looked for the pin in vain,
Shattered their heads with Hemingway's gun.
The season was fitting—like a mask.

I, in my grave, merely turned, fed the worms.

Tea

Speaking the language of strangers, spirits in the cup
Rise; steam is the essence of all brewing silence.
In a minute the tea will grow cold.
We consider its use in expressing our spent passion
For each other.
Or again, sit politely by the clogged sink
And marvel at the faces in it waiting
To be washed
Then walk back to tea, hand behind back
Grasping a kitchen knife, or such,
Thinking of the ruddy fountain locked in the jugular vein,
Thinking of the tea, a murder already halfway Dutch,
Thinking of the sea, froth, empathy,
Wanting to throw tea in each other's face
In a rush of epiphany;
Waiting to watch what tea did
To faces scared to look over the horizon of the cup
Into the wide, wild brimming nothing
Of the day and nothing speaks
But fumes the stone-cold tea
We will never, never drink.

Cargo

Of the mortifying body
You hold in your arms.
I am grateful to be of service
Like an old chair in a new house.

Beyond this young embrace,
The road combs the day's district
Great with transactions.

Across the street,
Shops hang up their trophies
Of tonic, toys, animal fat.
Stuff that atrophies.

And men returning
With money to meet their children
Newly risen from the Sun,
Its hours sought after a use.
How brittle our bones rest in bed.

Love, we don't know the how of this,
Its origin and end are beyond
The assurance planted by your kiss.
Deep the evening, into which the day sails slow
Like a ship bearing on its deck our residence.

Brief her lingering in the light
Even as we slip through our fingers, betraying.
We are part of the cargo.

Afterwards

Afterwards when the fallen days
Had thudded against each other under water
And settled down home to silence
We rose from the grass fiddling the air
The wild music to which lazily danced
The bestiary of the sky
We shook time out of our shoes
And walked
Towards the huge inverted cups
Of the hills where the old barn wore hay for hair
And was at ease with the blue vases at the back

Collecting night.

A tough old place where afterwards had arrived
And occupied its peace.
The furniture's whisper, like pouring sands,
Was hushed under the snowing covers.
The place in-between was ground
For mourning a generous prospective
Of breakfast and bed.

We fled the scene the same night
And once across the river, looked back.
The house was going up in a pyre of fireflies.
We held up a hand and blotted out the sight.

Forgetting the Dark

We were talking
About suffering
And van Gogh, his dark,
And the posthumous value
Of suicidal art
When the lights went out.
The air was thick
With mosquitoes
Like rumours.
Then one of us got up
To buy candles and remembered
Too late the lift wouldn't work
But he went down the steps
Anyway. We drank hard
And talked
Until he returned
In the dark
And paused at the open door panting.
He had been all over, he said.

We grew quiet while he lit the candles
Just as the power came back.
We were thrilled
Because all was light.
Meanwhile
We had forgotten van Gogh
And the dark.

Ghost

The day migrant, mirrors continents in little puddles
Over which fly birds to fair weather, friends.
Today in this house I am true to myself and numb
To music. Your footprints flavour a foreign soil, cold,
Ornamental, frosted white with October's breath.

Here the rain's gone, but for the drops you caught
In a blue bottle and left in a corner of the drawer
Like a lamp shining in a catacomb—months ago.
Tonight I move house and home to other margins.

I clear the drawers of snapshots, letters
The usual footnotes to future,
Read again, how through words course
The drift of a meaning. And by mail arrives
Little by little the map of a going.

If we could trace a line to its first wandering point
In a smile; see a word fully crystallize, all its meanings
Clear, we would be forever sending to each other
Post-cards explaining exactly what we hadn't meant.

I flush the papers down the tomb of the toilet—
A cistern transports as well as a ship—
And close the door in a face hard to recognize
If chanced upon again under water.

Whatever's left in there
Behind closed doors now
Must learn to keep its nerve
And drink alone the bottled rain.

Question: Do You Have Nightmares?

Answer: These roses which you sent are fine
Except that they grow
All the time. It's as if they feed
On the night of late strewn with a dead man's eyes
Which turn brighter by the minute
Like approaching headlights.
It's one week since the postman
Brought the flowers, and he,
A man given to picture postcards
And poetry, is due back here
For inspection the day after.
The forty-fourth day of the month
To be precise. This means
Not much time for me to retrieve
His terrorized glasses from
Amidst the fattening roses.
I need to cook some meat
For them. Then there's the question
Of that corpse upstairs; torn flesh
Bursting through buttons
That your gift must explain.

The Colours of the Season's Best Dream

My dear Doctor Hartman,

Not to put a fine point on it
Here in the city we drink
Chilled smog
And eat pickled soot.
We wear snakeskin suits
And our beauties this winter
Look like bruised fruit.
Don't ask us why.
This city is sly.

We plan to stay here
For as long as it takes,
Though the weather is a rogue.
We miss our village
We feel as if we are
From another age,
And truly we miss you
Our sage.

The trouble, as you know,
Is the hole
In our baby's heart.
No glue seems to play
Its part.

The baby, oh, the baby, doctor,
Flies birds out of his oriental eyes
And his fingers curl like burnt paper
And are light like ash in our hands.
Tonight a moon blooms in the mirror.
Trick or treat, it's blue like our baby's face.

Please visit us, Doctor Hartman,
When you have the time;
Tell us all this is a lie.
We will go back together,
The four of us.
I swear we won't cry.

Beauty

Beauty makes
My heart go tight.
It's the old Grecian Urn.
Got to break it
Beyond return
To keep it out of harm
From human sight.

What van Gogh Meant

To catch this evening's light
You need a van Gogh.
It's a flaming yellow billowing;
And how it transports the leaves
To a violent terminus of smudges.
An evening that can end
Only in one way.

The rumour that Lee is
No more Roger's wife
Has turned out to be true.
Roger just called
To say, yes, it's true.
Lee is involved with a Scot.
She is in Boston for a course.
She spoke to Roger on the phone
About the Scot who is nameless
But sweet.

Well, it looks like she has outgrown
Me, says Roger. There's nothing now
Between us, just this sea.
Roger is calling from a bar
In Bandra by the sea.

I can hear people talking
In the background.
I can even hear the sea
The other side of which is Lee.

In a letter to Theo,
A while before his suicide,
Van Gogh says he thinks he can now
Paint the sea.
I didn't know
What van Gogh meant
Till Roger's call about Lee.

Beauty Parlour

Surrounded by mirrors
You sit, waxed, tweezed
Plucked, fleeing ugliness
Through pain, hazarding,
From instruments of torture
A refuge from your face,
A beautiful guess.
Your hair is my rent.
Your wrinkles
My vacation.
I shall feed
To fat wrung
From rabbit tears
Your dry wrists.
Your sagging cheeks
Fuel my car.
Your double chin
And rock-like warts
Are my insurance.
Listen, the face you shed
And the one you grow
Are the two sides
Of a coin shining
Like a mirror
In which I see
My future
Fresh as mint.

Happily Living Ever Laughter

In public places like the morning
Where Sunday strolls, or the evening,
Parks, plazas, or pizzerias by the sea
And other such open spaces, I shall not
Go out to meet you, and watch you
Thin the crowd to a man, each one
Possessing you wholly with his eyes.
It's an act that dares murder
And is punishable by suicide.

So I lie in my bed, imagining—
Since this love cannot be for real—
A delirium for two, a coded speech,
That grants us exclusive possession
Of all space, summary silence to others.

Marine Drive

Execution by water's edge.
Sunset by the sea. Your hour.
The clock strikes catastrophe.
In the distance
Stout light's brief holding out,
Slow bleeding arteries of light.
Things burn
With a beauty from within.
Seance time when forms are free
To be fearless,
Free to return to provoke and punish.

Inhabit the incandescent hour
Measured by the sun-dial of the heart.
Tell stories to air and water
The legends of the shadows of the past.

Anti-clockwise all laughs.

Mirror in Blizzard When Lights Went Out

Cracked light. Gradations glow
In search of sight.
Captive
Of white milling around,
Peg to silence falling like snow,
Pensive as a peak
And clamped to the carpet,
Your eyes still fish for summer
In prismatic pools, parabolic streams
Drowned in a rush of eyes,
Bitten bullets,
The white weather gathered
In your metal hair.

Return in refracted measure
Their unforgiving stare. Even as a hand
Flickers, bear witness to your world
Falling apart in flakes.
Exiled from touch
Watch the vision vanish in reflection.

Starters

Harbingering fingers thrust
Into the celibate air
Instructions in ageing before time:
Morning mail perfumed, your letter.
Love, hate, regret and festive words
Of future scrape their heels off
Foreign lands.
Dislodged fragrance
Mingles with descending dust.
I imagine you marching out of a studious room
To the order of a colder light,
Having discovered a sort of happiness
In distance. Egress.
I reach for my first drink,
The fountain flowing out of my head,
Dark ink.

A Cold Feeling

Words are cold things, come after
Broken ties and slammed doors.

They form frost at the turning hour
When the mouth holds in a round stare
The loss that the dark piles behind the eyes
And no candle brings from the shade
All you've touched or read.

Sometimes I wake in this cold,
An icy sea winding over my head
Like a shroud. Words are old things
Come after much yearning,
When you no longer want what can't be had.

From *Gemini II*

Low Life

Click

He meets her at the bus stop,
A small, pretty woman
Who has decided early on
Not to want anything.
When he meets her,
He hears a camera go click.
She smiles. Click.
He offers her his seat.
Thank you, she says. Click.
The other day, they had tea together. Click.
All his moments with her were in snapshots,
Just for his wallet.
Never to be taken out.

———

Curios

It's three in the morning.
The house rings with alarms,
There's someone leaning
On the doorbell. It's her
After three years.
Her lets her in,
Puts on some tea.
She lights a cigarette
With a match that might set
The house on fire.

She unpacks the weather
Which is New York.
They sit in silence.
The room turns into a museum of moods.

A Friend in Need

He sits in a chair
Whose fourth leg's his.
He loves this chair.
They used to make love in it.
That was when the chair
Had four legs plus two,
Eight legs. Days with legs.
Since then there's been a lot of walking out.
Now the chair's short of a leg.
And he's lending his.

Shopping

In the shopping arcade the shutters
Come down between the stars
And the statues. The day's fashion
Catwalks into the cold.
The dark thickens the corners.
The mannequins are free
To collapse inside their suits, begin
Their nocturnal life, avenge the agony
Of iron postures. Ebony rude nudes.

Their hard laughs fall on the wet street
Like detached dentures. We lean
Stiffly on our last smiles, while
Our teeth trot in dismay to winter's
Wind. We are dying, love.
Gifts in our hands, we must part,
Open them in separate lands.

Catch-22

There were times when he didn't know
What to do with his love
Especially since she seemed
Quite all right without it.
At such times he drew the blinds
And closed the door
So the sun couldn't spot him
Nor anyone else.
In this blind fashion
He survived his love.
But his vision didn't improve.

Invisible Man

Every day
He felt his beard and thought
Of scissors
He could then write her about it.
So this morning

He was all set.
Well, the mirror broke

That's how he lost his face.

A Visit to the Countryside

The gurkha liked him.
One day
While watching TV together
The gurkha saw his village
Light up the room. Come
With me to my place, he said,
You will like it up there in the mountains,
It's not a wry place like this.
Only salt's hard to come by.
He looked himself in the eye
And thought about her.

Salt's no trouble, he said, let's go.

Milk Still Boils

He lies in bed, one hand
Thrown across his eyes.
This, he figures, is more like it.
He no longer thinks about her,
Or him. Just them.
And the postures they struck
Just before the milkman came.

In a minute he will be up
To put the milk on the boil
And none the wiser.

Morning Show

Everything there
Was a photo-story
Of something else
Except her face.
The way the books leaned
Against each other
Like friends caught in a crisis.
Under the cot, two dead sparrows.
Insurance details
Of a faceless former tenant.

All this he saw at a glance
In the early morning light
Brought from a night's journey.
Stills from a film
Whose title was her name.

So he drops anchor and waits.

Demolition

Fever pitches a tent high above my brow
And big enough. Dark dreams in one corner
Talk to each other of their recurring nature,
Ephemerality of sleep, delirium. In another,
Nameless sacrifices of dogs put up their nose
For missing masters. Ah, but in this anosmic weather!
Only water hurts like a shower of needles.

Nothing gives
Save the body its sweat, and the black cat
Her claims to tail. The joints ache in friendly disservice,
Helping the mind to toss precisely between
Image and vision. All in all, a house well-kept.

We stayed here for long enough to know
Our places in relation to each other.
Comfort was in the air like an old tale.
And then paracetamol
Brought the house down, and its inmates fled,
Looking for shelter, the bonhomie of fever.

Departure

Suspension of the wind, sloughing of the sun.

Natural wonders kept in abeyance
By the smoked glass,
And its numb reprisal which
Takes you away from me.

The second-hand weather facilitates
Our arrival to the parting point
Where we may kiss and forget the kiss.
And forget to sweat.
There's no snow inside here, but functional cold.
This lounge is for just what's possible.

Let's stop here. Take stock in silence
Of what may not be there any moment now.
Any further movement of the tongue
Will in time be tonsure of the heart,
The aching art of deliberate forgetting.
Or, at best, a generous selection
Of the details of our imperfection.

In time, our goodness may
Reconcile us to our failure
Perhaps exact from our separate nights
Mutual pardon for the transactions
Which brought us to this door.
But, irrespective of this moment
When we are quite finished,
See, love, how the birds take off for the sun
On eager wings like short-arms of the cross.

Roadshow

This was a while ago. One of the last nights
Of a summer long as the Ganges and most days
Filthy like some places by the river. You wished
To wash and dry them out in the moonlight.
This night had that kind of moon. A manic moon
Running amok, ready to grin and clean anything.

Then the pilot clouds of monsoon arrived.
Dark hair down. Tenebrae. And the lights went out, too.
Oh, twice tenebrae. It was like all the angels
Were down with animus.

At this point, when everything was about to weep
And our trust in each other flickered,
The Night Special came, bathed in neons,
Flush with fresh paint, an olfactory feast.
She lit our way
Into her bosom.

And we travelled the night in this fashion,
Swaddled in light, and watched the darkness shred.
We were glad of the mystery of this transport
And loved each other for some time to come.

Elusive

There's a face I look for everywhere,
Serene and still,
A blur of lines forming and dissolving,
Always a little beyond my vision
Like someone you knew to her last scent
From long ago, glimpsed as the hours darken
Between the chimes of two different clocks.
Or just missed like a beat,
Before the street band carried her
Leaving behind the impression
Of a glance that spoke to all of me,
Into the fluorescent crowd of the neon-night.
Or the pond envying the park's green
Whose water I part with running fingers
And see
That face flowering
And the next instant fade,
Become again the remote fragrance
That befriends and betrays me.

Renunciation

First light on the kitchen table
Breakfast for one. Beer and wine.
Feline eyes kiss fallen tart.

Lunch is a conceit of three. My cat,
Your snapshot and me. Secret rum
In mint tea. Invalidation of the sun.

Last light comes to sup. Dinner is a feat
In rectitude. Water and whiskey. Campaign
Of shadows on the wall. No despair.

A silver of music around the ankles.
Endless retreat of inaccessible feet.

Movie

Hands crossed, we watch
A Japanese movie
With different eyes,
But conscious of each image
Quivering like an arrow
In our heart.
This has been a difficult love
For the while it lasted;
What we feel
Is not what we speak
And in translation
We lose, just like these subtitles.
But the images remain.
Who knows, this night may be our last.
On the screen the lovers cry,
Our cheeks wet with their tears.

Sunrise in Bed

The grey deepens, cumulous beast
Edgeless in its expanse, spreads
Its misery's blind glare over
The fungal green of the deemed vase;
Denies grace of the dark, a place to hide.
The day stops at nothing, alters angles, scenes, plots;
Frames its friend the window with murder of the night,
Lifts the mask of the dark from the mould on scones,
Teases torture out of each object,
Touches the finger to light.
Crushing-close to the face
The wedding ring turns visible worm.

Retard

Morning once, my troubles, only teething,
The hour was a child laughing
At the crowded family weekend.

Friends and relatives came in droves.
Candies coloured the sun. In mangroves
Wild cousins blossomed and bent

To angles of ecstasy and dare.
The kitchen whistled round the clock.
Hair-raising aunts ordered pizzas on the phone.

Then the sun leapt and struck like a lion.
Each room exploded with the noon.
I saw my fairies and princes send

Their tales for other ends. These told upon
The house till it divided and each of us
Stood alone. Tall now,

I grope under the stones
For sweets, careful not to touch the bones.
I hold the old wrappers tight like a band

Over my eyes, hide from the terrors
That tend to the sun's growing pride.

Malabari

Out of My Window

June speaks thirty times
Each speech rhymes in green,
Praises water where it falls.
Leaves plunge yellow and brown
Stem the oozing mud with rotting colours.
Flakes of smokey light slip,
Branch by branch, through the spread-out noon.
In tall nests of foliage,
Thunder rests, gathers its throat
Often as not. Eaves sprint and scramble
Under the regal rain. Rugal earth.
Water strokes all, holds sepia
Close to green. Whispers in moist phrases
To the six cassocked nuns on the road
Who drily stare:
This mystery we bear.

Inspiration

Space shot with yellow,
April and May burn Malabar,
Laburnum's last coast.
Enter June, on long stilts of rain,
Putting out the fire in floral eyes
By its watery breath.
Brightness blinded.
Little ixora and jasmine

Nod their heads to the beating rain;
Tremble for the peace between two blows
Remembering laburnum,
The firmness of that flame.

Zamorin

I, king of all the sea I see,
Hold you, love, fair as the desert
From where you come, and the fire your god,
More dear than the black stone
On which I sat to be crowned
(The one that the British stole
And carried to Cochin, home
To another thief);
That stone is yours. Also the rain
And its lashes. When the whip of water
Tires, let my tears take its wet place.
This is the chill purpose of my rule.
Yours the kingdom.

Piscina

At Feroke, where the river meets the sea
All is green outside my feet, sheathed
In the light of refracted palms, except
The chaos of silver, the pale, pale
Floss of fish that dart through
Two destinies.

When they congregate under water
Their stillness is like a prayer.
When cat-blobs of rain fall and claw
The surface, they separate in search
Of haven.

Nothing stomachs such ravenous greetings
Like the two fish-speaking waters of Malabar,
Negrito land swimming in green,
Always in the eye even if unseen.

———

Legacy

Abdication of the unreal at night; crowning
Of home truths. The house surrenders easily
To the walls, trapping the sleeping dead
Into recesses, where no hand shines. Flotsam
In personal seas out of mutual reach.
Each to his riches: inarticulate vagaries,
Inversion, exclusive madness, inclement seasons
Of the heart. Wild game on the wall
Hold in their ornate gaze the hall in thrall
With speechless, final visions:
Stories of steel, speed and blood.

Up in the attic, nocturnal communion.
Ancestral spirits rasp the mercy of the whip
And the sword in a foreign language; pitch
Their losses and fears like sails into the memories
Of the dying, continue their search
For a posthumous purpose.
Tableau evenings, music of the tribe and cattle calls
From an age over the hill throng the dispossessing dark.

Through the monumental air, closed doors,
Endless corridor of faint recalls and wet wind,
You wander, love, an image taming estranged space,
Daring the multitudes of salt-sadness.

Sunday Morning Jerk Off

No oranges, no complacencies
Of the peignoir. Heel in my hand,
I outstare the sole of the beast
Twisting in my fist, shedding shape.

This bed. Perhaps this bed is all.
No lines, not a shadow breaks its plainness,
A calligraphy of distance, not of this soil.
A blind padding of flesh, upon which
I move or rest, but always
The arrogant measure of earth.

My foot on her face,
The face privy to all pedigree
To its first root.
This bed. Perhaps this bed is all.

Annunciation

Room temperature if unlit. Otherwise hot.
Dread coal. Bituminous
Or anthracite; but shining stone
In deep disguise. Queer agate;
Blackened eye of battles; turns blood to soot,
Idles in the dark till all sweat is salt.
Gives nose to iron, makes it move; bites the eye.
The eye that can see.

I watch it burn, and the cold keeps away from me,
Fading with the white breath of mountains
I cannot see. Rake the bloody lot if you must.
But take care: they sprung roots once,
Held earth in place. Played with bones,
Toyed with the sea, before they burnt like this,
Confiding to the air their consuming craft.
Like my love. If it is to be, it must burn
And be no more.

Annunciation II

Place of perpetual solar suicide,
Cordoned off by precise fears. In your street
The hour is always wild sunset. And in some clock
Somewhere, I too am dead.

You turn your face, the dead man turns with you.
You run, he is in step with you. A shadow
In your eyes, the dead man dies with you.
You shout, flout, use and abuse.
Hate, deny, drawback, mock.
Smile, hold, release: a configuration
Of dry tears, beautiful bones, a body
Built for unearthly torture. Ascension
At the thirteenth hour, when all clothes fall

And involuntary powers walk the earth.
I reach out, touch and let go;
Not caring if this is a birth
Or a seasonal death you lend, borrow?

Witch

At the chorusing hour in the morning,
Wind prodding rain, the first bus ploughing
Water, painted cattle plodding knifeward
And a hint of light rimming the room,
I rise, and pass
In and out of a foreign land rampant
With surprises: you do not resist.
At the last entrance, I die carefully,
Crying out your name, a password
For the world to momentarily desist.

Loose Ends

Standing hunched in the evening light,
The kitchen reflects on the silence
Of the saucers serving time in the sink; jars
Brooding over their spent space; the clouded mirror
Gathering cowled forms of the night,
Falling stars, dust, and detects an absence.

The walls are a conspiring
Witness to your despair:
A line from Donne on saints.
Another, from Neruda, shivers blue
Like a dart gone home to rue.
Above the stove cold as your last bow
Hangs Shergill's Nude, wooing solitude.

To the left of the mirror, spreads in suspended rage
Cornfields—trapped in the winds
Howling out of van Gogh's eyes—waiting
For the birds to forswear flight, fall.
Upon the fridge, limp lie milkman's wages,
Laundry bills, pills. And in a corner of the room,

Swirl like a storm a few pages of your scattered rage.

First Signs, Last Rites

The air thrums. What restored aches, basalt
Landscapes sternly rise with the sun,
Deciding the direction of the spirit's flair
For self destruction. On the cross
Mercy twists; offers salvation in the farrago flesh.
The five wounds stare in the eye of the god
They cannot understand. The same sands
Shift the hours.

It must be like this then. This dereliction
Of the senses, made inscrutable by hands
Ever washing the water red.
Broken bread; stale wine.

Three bells
And the newspaper falls at your feet.
I count the casualties of the circuit
Of whirling insects and men

And wait in the packed train
For the wasting away of the unsung flesh.

Requiem of the Rose

1.

Blazon in the sky: offers a centre,
Blazing consolation to vultures drowning
Upward on the sly. It's noon again, when forms
Lose shape, lie. Brace yourself
Against the tawny gravel, entranced lamp-posts,
Shimmering windows closed to communion,
Hacked earth shifting in the haze like a lion's mane
And the ebony cascade of the road along which
She will go and you also; what's left of the day
Burning in your pocket
In the flowers she wore yesterday.

2.

Progress towards the centre. Suffer exclusion
Like a door. Answer none, save the knock out of turn.
Watch out for rust, cracks, false key in the lock.
Swear by silence not to belong. The moment is blind,
Lacks reference. You have stolen its eye, you witness.
Gaze into the noon through a veil of guile. Be the sun.

Lazarus

Long after sleep's slow fade out,
The dream lay in his eyes, heavy
Like a sandy landscape in rain;
An angular place without a name,
Looking up at the sky.
Blood counted for nothing here. And, so,
He joylessly surrendered himself to murder,
Incest, adultery as also theft
And polar arrogance.
A land locked
By its own acts, all justified
And no questions asked. He could not err
And be condemned to another's forgiveness
Here. Nothing escaped its jealous gravity,
Not a word. A flawless solitude. Its perfection
Paled the bejouterie of his tears.
When it was time, he wore dark shades
And became one with the crowd.

Back

I return by mirror to the same light
Playing with grime on the dull steelware
And the mothballs wasting away
In the witchery of their fumes, like a crime.
The kitchen has grown colder by a lightyear. A polite
Place for poltergeist and blight.

The fan still spins in the spoon, though.
I am grateful for this comfort. But the stove
Doesn't light and the tap refuses to turn.
Stealth stifles the air; the house conspires.

Home, I tell the man turning away in the mirror.
My captive. Let him go?
Cut my wrist and set off a little sunset.
Let him go.

Saturday Poems

War

Shit scared he sits, wishing
Monday were here.
There's no fooling the weekend though.
He looks in the fridge,
The snow falling on sausages.
He counts his bottles, fingers crossed.
He boils water by the gallons
To beat death by cholera
On a weekend binge.
He avoids the mirror
For fear of being watched.
He draws the blinds
And lets in the dark, glass at hand.

Saturday's ready for war.

Travel

He sits in his solo chair
Like a heap of potatoes.
He doesn't care for the sun
Burning the day down like wax.
He ignores the window,
The double-deckers
And their riders below.
He's busy focussing his eyes

On the table, carrying his sixth drink
Like a patient waiter.
He needs to put on his socks
And go far from his feet.

Harmony

Fallen eggs and smoking pans;
Yellow the floor. Toppled sugar
Spreads mutiny
Among ants. The flies feast
On the visible. Invisible
Their purpose. The one-eyed
House lizard turns transparent
In its intent. His cat's on the fridge
Watching the world unfold:
So many meals cooking in the kitchen.

Marked

Result of much confession, the secret glances;
Shining from shared heaviness of the mind,
That light touch. At night the relief of being
Together, after near-fatal wanderings, the closed door
Like a sentinel steadfast, and flesh's yielding
Assurances; at times the wake into the rain talking,
And the laziness of the first tea are hours exiled.

Their absence recommends neither regret nor
Celebration, but the observance of a pose or two:
Stares blind with distance, left hand consulting
The face without conclusion. Of a Sunday morning
I rest my head on the sleeping stove,
Breathing in the steel's hard fragrance. Stricken
And preserved in such postures, I constantly think
Of the need for a new distortion,
And let its satisfactions disfigure my face.

Documentary

A benevolence of lights arching over
The proceedings lent her skin the right
Texture. When he said 'action', fresh blood
Braved her old veins. And she was ready again
With the folklore of an extinct tribe.

She played her parts well: a captive tortured
By her own famous talents; ballerina who
Practised rigor mortis at the sight of love's talons;
Cross-bred babe of six languages, vague words;
Sweat-breaking glazed ceramic mother
Ending the act before things got over.
They were pleased by her instant returns
To seasons of make-believe, her efforts
To make a home out of an intact habit;
She almost became her painted face.
Then the past passed her by once again.

Dire

1.

If simplicity, plain mud and, its future, stone,
Were the end, I have seen it with my eyes:
The thinning blood, thickening water.
All entangling knots of touch, sound
And the trespassed ground, roll back to rock;
All sweet-blooded intent, killed as soon as it is born
By this skill of my occult eyes,
From which there is no release. This too
Is a gift; invokes desolation, like unappeased faith.

2.

Thus pleasure dies; the jolly, wrong thing
Rare as love without purpose.
The phallus turns a fossil; desire wilts
In the dispiriting presence of omniscience.
(But Poseidon, that night still burns like a torch
In the brooding air following me through
Every tick of time).

3.

Something must be wrong
With the very first word, the hyoid bone.
Avoid me; learn to hide.
I am the stare. You are the stone.

Stranded

Listening to voices breaking, doors closing
Glass smashing, traffic moving,
Tears welling, sea heaving;
Watching movies, birds rising, women walking,
Children reading, hands holding, lips parting,
Days passing, fields flying;
Inhaling books, linen, hair, body secrets
And the rain arriving;

He stood, rooted to the spot.

Immortals

They breathed the same air as we did; watched
The rain grow back to air as grass; starlight churn
Green in the eyes of cats; sat and held a dying hand,
Perhaps wept restoring it to the relinquishing heart.
Or paced shadow-striped lawns, and paused mid-stride,
Startled by a thought that cleared the air for all. Wrote;
Or wrought, with brush, or metal; turned the tide.
Had a mind that went around the universe like a wrap
And bound the stars. Those who walked by the miracle
Of dawn, charted the crystal-map of grief in a drop
Of sun-splintering tear; swam over the moon in water,
Drank themselves in their solitude to a daze
And finally turned, like the rest of us, to dust:
Salutes to their unwavering, shaping gaze.

Acknowledgements

Akshaya Pillai, who nudged me back into poetry, when I thought it was over for me.

Dibyajyoti Sarma and Raghavendra Madhu for painstakingly formatting the poems, and often typing them in when software failed.

Kanishka Gupta for selling the idea of *Available Light* to Ravi Singh.

Ravi Singh for buying the idea.

Radhika Shenoy for working through the draft despite a bad back to meet a cruel deadline.

My reliable dreams.

ALSO IN SPEAKING TIGER POETRY

FULL DISCLOSURE
NEW AND COLLECTED POEMS (1981-2017)

Manohar Shetty

'Here is a book worth celebrating: Manohar Shetty's *Full Disclosure: New and Collected Poems (1981-2017)*, which gathers more than thirty years of work from a major voice in world Anglophone poetry. More accurately, this book presents a range of voices—in some of the multi-sectioned poems a choir—as Shetty writes through a variety of personae and perspectives, delivering emotionally resonant deep imagery and intellectual precision, profound compassion and ironic wit, in equal parts.... This collection provides us with a broad survey of a celebrated poet's past and present while offering an enticement for his—and our—future.'

–John Hennessy,
poetry editor of *The Common*

www.ingramcontent.com/pod-product-compliance
Lightning Source LLC
Chambersburg PA
CBHW051112230426
43667CB00014B/2553